SICK!

The Twists and Turns Behind Animal Germs

SICK!

The Twists and Turns Behind Animal Germs

Heather L. Montgomery

illustrated by

Lindsey Leigh

BLOOMSBURY
CHILDREN'S BOOKS
NEW YORK LONDON OXFORD NEW DELHI SYDNEY

BLOOMSBURY CHILDREN'S BOOKS
Bloomsbury Publishing Inc., part of Bloomsbury Publishing Plc
1385 Broadway, New York, NY 10018

BLOOMSBURY, BLOOMSBURY CHILDREN'S BOOKS, and the Diana logo
are trademarks of Bloomsbury Publishing Plc

First published in the United States of America in February 2024
by Bloomsbury Children's Books

Bloomsbury Publishing Plc does not have any control over, or responsibility for,
any third-party websites referred to or in this book. All internet addresses given in
this book were correct at the time of going to press. The author and publisher regret
any inconvenience caused if addresses have changed or sites have ceased to exist,
but can accept no responsibility for any such changes.

This book is for information purposes only and does not make any medical recom-
mendations. Readers should not try medical experiments at home!

Bloomsbury books may be purchased for business or promotional use. For information on bulk purchases please contact Macmillan Corporate and Premium Sales
Department at specialmarkets@macmillan.com

Library of Congress Cataloging-in-Publication Data
available upon request
ISBN 978-1-5476-0985-7 (hardcover) • 978-1-5476-0986-4 (e-book) • 978-1-5476-0987-1 (e-PDF)

Interior design by Kay Petronio

Printed and bound in China by C&C Offset Printing Co Ltd, Shenzhen, Guangdong
2 4 6 8 10 9 7 5 3 1

To find out more about our authors and books visit www.bloomsbury.com
and sign up for our newsletters.

In memory of
Grandma Feather
and
Grandma Martin,
who gifted me with
a passion for biology
and the willpower
required to write
this book.

CONTENTS

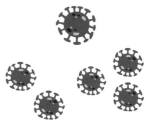

SICK!

The Twists and Turns Behind Animal Germs

RNING

- This **IS NOT** a textbook. Don't expect neat chapters with tidy explanations. Are you okay with unanswered questions?

- This **IS NOT** an encyclopedia. There's imagination at play in these pages. Are you ready to sort the fact from the fancy?

- This **IS NOT** an average info book. These stories have been selected to take you to a place you've never been. Are you willing to let your mind be blown?

This **IS** science in action!

Animals Under Attack

**PROJECTILE PUKE,
SHOWERS OF SNOT,
DAYS OF DIARRHEA.**

At one time or another, we've all experienced some sick symptoms. And we've all dreaded that one word: **INFECTED!!**

Infections are icky. Infections are tricky. Infections are caused by pathogens. When a pathogen is microscopic, some people call it a germ. When it is not, some people call it a parasite. Whatever you call them, everybody knows organisms that infect human bodies are bad, bad, bad.

Right?

After all, a germ's got a job:

ATTACK. INVADE. DESTROY.

How do they do it?

STEP 1: Concoct a sneaky strategy to get inside. They might . . .

slide up the slime inside a nose,

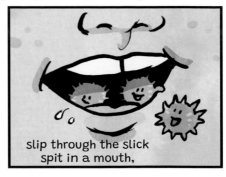

slip through the slick spit in a mouth,

weasel their way through a crusty crack in the skin,

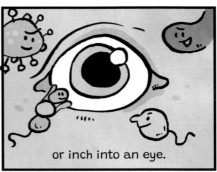

or inch into an eye.

STEP 2: Hack, whack, and smack through the body's infection fighters.

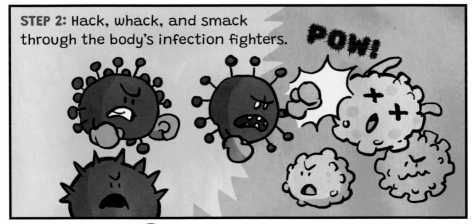

POW!

STEP 3: Turn the body into a squirmy germy factory to pump out pathogen after pathogen after pathogen!

Ever since ancient times, germs have done a pretty good job with their job. You might have experienced some entirely inconvenient effects of pathogens—like puke, pus, or pounding headaches. But sometimes pathogens cause more than that . . .

When a super sickness lands on the land, when a parasite becomes more than a pest, when an infection ignites an epidemic, what's a body to do?

Your body is an *animal* body, so why not ask the animals?

When it comes to tiny attackers infecting their bodies, animals have got a few tricks to put those pathogens in their place. Some of those tricks rely on microscopic molecules:

Time for my secret weapon!

SLIME!!

Hagfish slime doesn't just gum up shark gills . . .

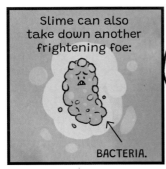

Slime can also take down another frightening foe:

BACTERIA.

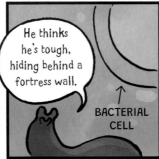

He thinks he's tough, hiding behind a fortress wall.

BACTERIAL CELL

Hagfish slime's got lysozymes for that.

Lysozymes are the perfect fit. So they can . . .

CRACK!

OR . . .

CRUNCH!

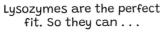

So water can rush in

through the holes.

KABLAM!

He, heheh!

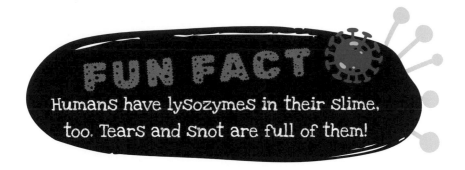
Some animal tricks call for a mom to step in to save her kids.

Mommy trick: *Disinfect it!* Mama monkeys pick their babies clean. Leopards lick their babies clean. But dogs may have the most daunting cleaning protocol of all.

Puppy poop can be packed with squirmy wormy parasites. No one wants that lying around the den, but it's especially dangerous for newborn pups. Their immune system—including a team of microscopic minions—hasn't developed yet. The mother has got to do something!

She doesn't have a pooper-scooper. No doggy doody bags. There's only one thing she can do: open wide and gobble up the poopy goop. Her immune system can take it—probably. Later, when she's away from the den, she'll take a squat and deposit those parasites far from her little ones.

WORD NERD

IMMUNE SYSTEM: a network of molecules, cells, and organs . . . that protects the body from outside invaders such as bacteria, viruses, and fungi.

Don't go thinking these moms are being lovey-dovey. It is all about ensuring that their DNA passes on down to the next generation.

DNA = twisted strands of code that sit quietly inside every animal cell and provide instructions. DNA carries segments of code called genes. Genes determine an animal's characteristics like hair color, body shape, and floppiness of ears. But DNA does more than create the cuteness of a koala. Genes give a baby's body the 411 for survival. And survival of babies is what keeps a species kickin'.

Ever since Kingdom Animalia got started, animals have been evolving wide-ranging ways to battle bad guys. Animals with successful adaptations have survived, reproduced, and passed their successful genes on to their young. Animals with weaker adaptations died off. That's how natural selection works. It pushes a population to evolve the strongest traits.

Why, then, are we so surprised to learn that a house mouse self-isolates when it's feeling kind of sickly? That bees fumigate their hive with the same pine-smelling chemicals we clean with? That tadpoles wiggle away from a contagious crowd?

Maybe it's because animals don't show off their behaviors or because pathogens are so skilled at staying hidden. Maybe it's because we haven't had the tools to look closely enough or because we weren't looking at the right things. Or maybe, just maybe, we haven't always been *open* to the possibilities.

Whatever the reason, all this awesome has been concealed under a cloak of invisibility.

It's time to pull off that cloak. Who can do that?

Scientists can!

Let's lean in and look. We'll start with a parasite large enough to see, then shrink smaller and smaller, down to a virus. Be prepared to see science sleuths in action, to marvel at the miracle of mammals, *and* to discover that a germ's got a gigantic job.

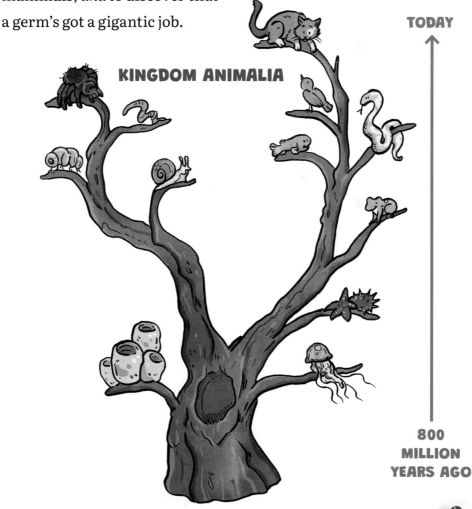

KINGDOM ANIMALIA

TODAY

800 MILLION YEARS AGO

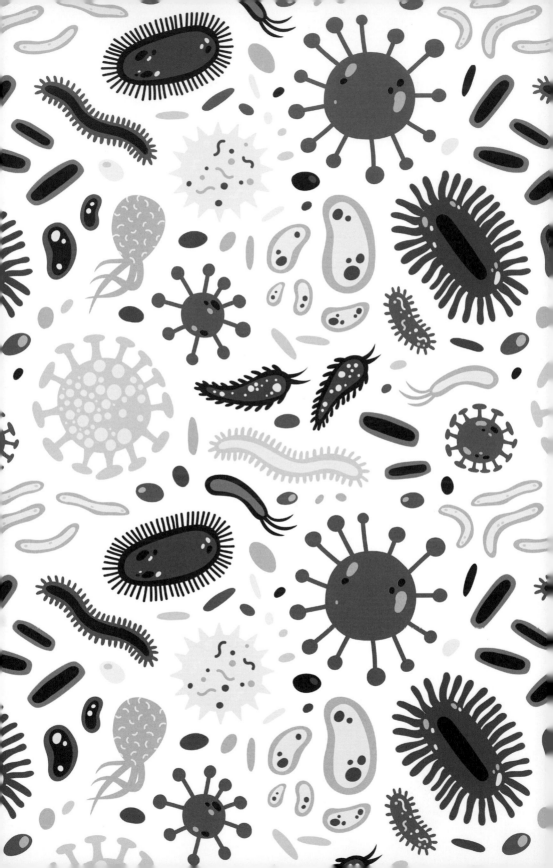

CHAPTER 1
A Chimpanzee Pharmacy

It all started on a November day way back in 1987, when Mike Huffman (a scientist from Japan) and Mohamedi Seifu Kalunde (a healer from Tanzania) squatted on a leafy mountain in Tanzania. They watched a chimp named Chausiku sit in front of a shrub, snap off stems, and peel them like bananas.

Snip. Snip. She bit small bites.

Crunch. Crunch. She munched it to mash.

Slurp. Slurp. She sucked out the sap.

Ptui. She spat out the tough stuff.

Chimps eat fruit, they eat leaves, they even swipe seeds from their own poop, but that plant, *mjonso*? Not so much. In the ten months Mike had spent becoming one with the chimps, he had never seen that.

Even the people of the local village (who sometimes swallowed mjonso to cure an upset stomach) said, "Bleeck! Too bitter!" No chimp would want to eat that.

FUN FACT

Some plants make bitter chemicals to keep animals from munching them. Those chemicals can also overpower germs—that's why people use them as medicine.

Something clicked in Mike's brain.

Was the chimp sucking the sap as medicine?

Chausiku *had* been acting odd. When her infant dangled dangerously high in a tree, she hadn't rushed to the rescue. When teenage chimps teased and tickled her tot, she hadn't badgered those bullies. When it seemed she should be comforting her little one, she just folded branches into a bed, flopped down, and lay there looking listless. Was she sick?

How could Mike know?

You can't walk up to a wild chimp and pop a thermometer in her mouth. You can't count on her to kindly swab both nostrils. You can't give her a cup to take to the toilet. Instead, Mike took notes and collected clues.

SCRIBBLE. SCRIBBLE. SCRIBBLE.

Her walk was slow and stiff. She hardly ate anything. She kept stopping and making herself beds in the middle of the day.

Mike and Mohamedi watched her pee: her urine looked too dark. They watched her squat: doo-doo barely dribbled out. Her odd behavior lasted all afternoon and into the next morning.

FUN FACT

Chimps pee and poop right off the sides of their daybeds!

Later that day, though, when all the chimps were taking a nap, Chausiku suddenly jumped to her feet and bolted. When her kid couldn't keep up, she pounded the ground, grunted, and kept going.

For fifteen minutes, she loped along on her knuckles. Mohamedi and Mike followed at a trot. Branches whacked their faces. Thorns grabbed their arms. Vines forced them to belly crawl.

Up, up, up, and down. Across one mountain. Across a second mountain . . .

Where was Chausiku going? Why was she going? What made her move so fast?

Mike had to know.

When he finally caught up to her, Chausiku was sitting in a swampy spot, popping food into her mouth—figs, ginger, and elephant grass. For more than two hours, she stuffed her face. She must have been feeling better!

Mike mulled over his observations. When humans take mjonso to cure crummies in their tummies, it works in 24 hours. He counted up the hours since Chausiku ate the plant: 23.

Had Mike just become the first person to document a chimp self-medicating? Mike's hunch turned into a hypothesis.

PARASITES APLENTY

What kind of sickness could have shut down the chimp? Take a look at her hand-washing habits and you might find some clues. Out there in the forest, there's no soap at the sink. Um, there is no sink!

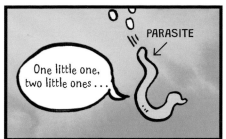

It's an open invitation for an internal parasite. Like a hookworm.

Hookworms are blood-sucking vampires. They worm their way into the small intestine and hack a hole in the organ's slimy lining.

My magical molecules keep the bloody juice flowing!

In some areas, 72 percent of black bears carry these babies.

Or a tapeworm.

Tapeworms have heads full of horrendous hooks. They latch on to animal intestines, then slurp in the slurry straight through their skin.

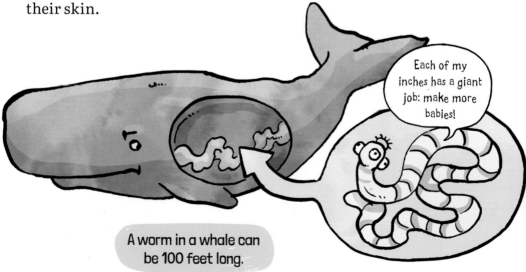

Each of my inches has a giant job: make more babies!

A worm in a whale can be 100 feet long.

Or a nodular worm.

A nodular worm might not look like much, but they're tough! Remove all their water and 20 percent of them manage to survive 6 months!

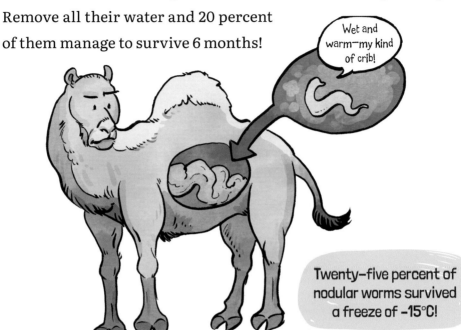

Wet and warm—my kind of crib!

Twenty-five percent of nodular worms survived a freeze of –15°C!

Any of these creepy-crawlies would be happy to hole up inside a chimp. So, there's no question, Chausiku *could* have had a wormy infection. But did she?

FUN FACT

Some sophisticated macaques have learned to wash their hands—at least the girls have— and are rewarded with fewer worms.

Mike knew where to find that answer. He dug through her dung. Sitting in all that squish, he found a worm,

Oesophagostomum stephanostumum. What a mouthful. Let's call him Oscar.

Hi, I'm a nodular worm.

Oscar likes to lodge in the wall of a small intestine. In a chimp, his happy homemaking might cause an ulcer, weight loss, or diarrhea.

Imagine your insides filled with lumpy bumps, each filled with one worm. Yuck.

Sometimes Oscar and his BFFs lie low, trying to avoid a fight. If the host never notices them, that's a win for the worms. Other times, Oscar fails to latch on to the intestine, so the chimp wins. But there's a third possibility: if Oscar and his friends do settle in and then they're detected, the chimp's body will fight back. Mighty warriors of the chimp's immune system—macrophages, neutrophils, antibodies—stream toward the intruder. Soon, the place is packed. The tissue swells. It turns hot and fills with pus. The battle bulges into an inflamed mass.

UNTIL . . .

UNTIL . . .

UNTIL . . .

The mass might rupture, dumping a toxic spew into the chimp's innards.

Oscar and all that inflammation can actually kill a chimpanzee.

Maybe Chausiku was trying to get rid of Oscar?

MORE POO CLUES

When Mike found worms in Chausiku's poo, it was a pretty strong clue. But one piece of evidence is not enough, so he kept digging for more. Back in his office in Japan, he read books and articles and everything he could find about sick critters. He read that other scientists had observed another odd chimp behavior—leaf swallowing.

It wasn't mjonso they were swallowing, it was *Aspilia*, a different plant. Could this be a different kind of chimp medicine?

A chimp would carefully pluck a leaf, fold it, and lay it flat on his tongue.

GULP.

He'd fold another. *Gulp.*

And another . . .

No chewing, just folding and gulping up to 100 leaves!

In all the reading Mike was doing, he spotted another hypothesis: Aspilia contains some kind of worm-killing drug.

Now this was an intriguing idea . . . Could this be a silver bullet to take down parasites? Could chimps teach us a cure?

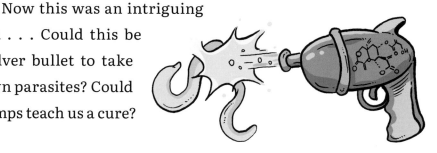

NOT-SO-FUN FACT

Over 3,000,000,000 people are infected with pesky parasites. Ones we can catch from chimps: giardia, animal scabies, or amebiasis. Those could give you foul farts, chew through your skin, or fill your brain with pockets of pus.

Mike was determined to find out. So, with a new mission in mind, back to Africa he went.

One day he followed a chimpanzee who was acting strangely. The chimp had been leaf swallowing. Knowing he needed to find some clues, Mike collected her poo. Would he discover parasites— or not? Unfortunately, that night Mike felt awful! Had he caught a bug from the chimp?

Once he was back on his feet three days later, Mike put his tweezers to work on the poo.

Pick. Pluck. Plop. PEEEE-EW.

There, in the middle of a turd, was a stack of *Aspilia* leaves. Not ground up. Not mashed up. An entire wad had come through untouched. Normally when a mouth munches on a leaf, it crunches through the tough fibers, then the gut goes to work digesting the food to release nutrients, energy, and other molecules.

If the leaves weren't crunched, they probably weren't food. If they weren't digested, how could any miracle drug have been released?

Mike tweezed the wad apart. There, squiggling and squirming between the leaves, were worms.

Wait a minute. Three days in a plastic baggie with these *supposedly* killer leaves and the worms weren't dead?

So much for the silver bullet idea.

Hey, get me outta here!

If the leaves weren't food . . . and they didn't have any magical worm-killing molecule . . . why would a chimp swallow a packed-leaf pill?

Mike thought. Mike taught. Mike talked to scientists across the globe. People started telling him stories. One researcher had seen white-handed gibbons in Thailand swallow leaves in a similar way. Someone else had spotted gorillas in the act. And still others found folded leaves in bonobo poo. Did those bonobos swipe the trick from their cousins, the chimps?

FUN FACT

Before brown bears hibernate, they swallow leaf wads. Before snow geese migrate, they lip smack packs of grass. Scientists have spied over 10 different species who swallow leaf wads.

Looking very closely at that chimpanzee poo, Mike noticed something. In every case, the leaves had tiny, bristly hairs.

Imagine gulping that down your gullet.

S-C-R-A-A-A-A-P-E!

Mike and his colleagues tracked more leaf-swallowing chimps. The animals seemed to do it in the morning, when their tummies were empty. Normally food wanders along, taking 23–48 hours to find its way through a chimp's system. But 6 hours later, these chimps were squirting poo and parasites. That's fast!

Mike's new hypothesis: the prickly leaves irritate an empty stomach, causing the gut to quickly flush the mass, scraping worms right off the intestinal wall and dumping them out of the body.

How do chimps learn which plants work as medicine? Do they know when they have worms? Is Mike's hypothesis right?

We still have lots of questions about chimp self-medication. But after thirty years of study, fifty publications, and hundreds of observations, Mike has a pretty good idea that chimps know what they are doing.

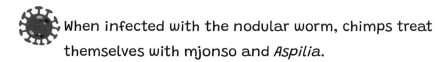

When infected with the nodular worm, chimps treat themselves with mjonso and *Aspilia*.

After one chimp slurped the bitter sap of mjonso, the number of worm eggs in a gram of its dung dropped from 130 to 15.

When chemists ground up mjonso they discovered 13 compounds new to science! Compounds that might terminate:

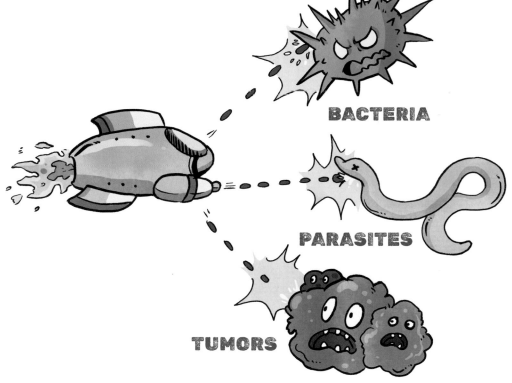

BACTERIA

PARASITES

TUMORS

Take that, you animal-attackers!

Maybe a chimpanzee's self-medicating abilities shouldn't surprise us. Chimps are smart enough to learn words, solve problems, and even beat people on a memory test. They are primates, after all, and our close cousins.

Lay out our DNA side by side with that of a chimp, and it's a 98 percent match.

What other ways do animals ward off attacks? Instead of popping pills, giant bustard birds pop blister beetles into their mouths—beetles that contain a toxin strong enough to blister skin. Inside the bird, the toxin zaps parasites and bacteria. If we keep our eyes and minds open like Mike does, we might learn more from our animal friends.

CHAPTER 2

A Frog and a Fever

Deep in the cloud forest of Panama, Cori Richards-Zawacki had her eye on a frog. A neon-yellow frog with bright eyes, black marks, and dashing good looks.

Sneak, snatch, grab—she got it! She marked the frog by clipping a bit from its toe, then released it.

Cori was concerned. People had been plucking the Panamanian golden frog from the forest—one pet, two pets, three pets—causing the population to plummet. So Cori started catching and counting frogs to answer a question: how many frogs could be taken before the population would collapse?

Over a couple of hours, Cori caught, marked, and released 15 golden frogs. While she had a frog in her hand, she recorded all kinds of information—their size and sex and body temperature and whether they were hanging out by the creek or up on the bluffs.

During that 2005 trip, Cori couldn't have known how

valuable that info would be. She couldn't see the swarm of spores swimming its way across Central America toward Panama. She couldn't guess the fate those frogs were about to face.

A FATAL FUNGUS

When you hear the word *fungus*, you might think of mushrooms. But a mushroom is just the fruiting part of a fungus (like the apple on a tree). A mushroom is the part we most often see, but fungi are way more than those funky, floppy pizza toppings.

Fungi aren't plants. They can't make their own food.

Fungi aren't animals. They can't even ingest food.

Fungi are so hard to categorize that they get an entire kingdom to themselves. Those in Kingdom Fungi feed themselves by spewing enzymes into the environment around them. When those enzymes make contact with wood,

ENZYMES (IHN zyms) = proteins that speed up reactions (in this case, the digestion of food).

soil, flesh, and more, they turn the material into usable nutrients that the fungi can suck up through root-like hyphae.

Formula for a fungus:

HUNGRY HYPHAE + ENERGETIC ENZYMES = SUPER SPORES

The nutrient-absorbing hyphae mostly stay hidden underground or inside bodies.

You can't see them, but fungal spores are everywhere! Right now, fungal spores are sitting on this book, drifting down onto your skin, or being sucked up into your nostrils. And thank goodness they are. Many fungi are our friends. Bread, yogurt, and soy sauce are just a few foods brought to you by our fungal BFFs. More importantly, fungi dine on dead bodies. Yes, that's a good thing: Imagine if trees never decomposed. The place would get pretty crowded.

SPORES

HYPHAE

But fungi aren't always friendly to us or to our four-legged friends. Meet *Batrachochytrium dendrobatidis*. Let's call it Bradley Bd. Bd is commonly called the amphibian chytrid fungus. It causes chytridiomycosis, which may be the most deadly animal disease on our planet. And Bradley Bd has his sights set on some unsuspecting frogs.

FUNGAL INVASION

Amphibians of Earth, prepare to be annihilated!

What? You think you can take us?

Just me and a few...

of my friends.

Last one in is a rotten egg!

Mine! All mine!

FROG CELL

And now, my little ones...

Go forth and conquer!

What does this Bradley Bd do to an animal? Cause oozing sores, painful pits, and revolting rot in the skin. That would be awful enough for a mammal, but for an amphibian, it is even worse. That's because amphibian skin is like a Swiss Army knife; it's multipurpose.

When Flavio Frog needs

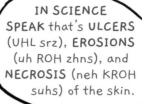

IN SCIENCE SPEAK that's ULCERS (UHL srz), EROSIONS (uh ROH zhns), and NECROSIS (neh KROH suhs) of the skin.

 to drink,

 to cool down,

 or to breathe,

skin's got that covered.

FUN FACT

Glands in the skin of poison dart frogs brew up a concoction of defensive proteins. Scientists are trying to swipe them to use in a vaccine against the flu.

On top of that, Flavio's skin controls the flow of electrolytes. Since a frog can't grab a sports drink to quench his thirst, his super-selective skin gives a green light to the right electrolytes instead.

Normally, tiny pores in his skin let in sodium and chloride (two important electrolytes). When the chytrid fungus comes along, it plugs up those pores. If his electrolytes get out of whack, Flavio's muscles can't take it. Bad news for the body's main muscle—

ELECTROLYTES = minerals (like sodium and potassium) in the body that carry an electrical charge.

FUN FACT

After you sweat, you might crave something salty. That's your body begging for electrolytes.

HEART ATTACK!

And Bradley doesn't stop after slaying a single Flavio.

Ah, springtime! The birds are chirping, the bees are buzzing.

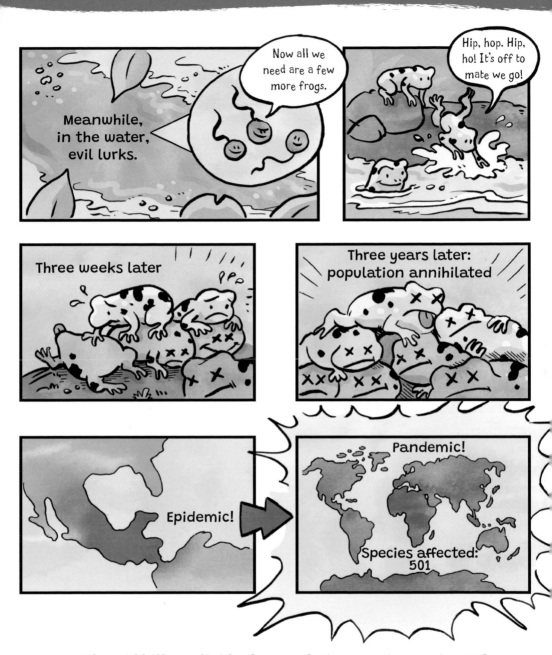

Chytrid kills. Individuals, populations, entire species. When the frogs are all dead and there is nothing left but decomposing bodies, that's extinction. Chytrid has caused the extinction of 90 frog species.

Will any frogs survive?

PLOTS AND PATTERNS

After Bd blew through Panama, Cori tripped and tromped back into the forest to see how that population of golden frogs was doing.

Cori found:

January 2005
Frogs Found: 123
Frogs infected: 0

December 2005
Frogs Found: 141
Frogs infected: 19

January 2006
Frogs Found: 200
Frogs infected: 94
Dead: 8

Things were looking bad. No one could figure out how to stop chytrid. No one knew much, but Cori did. Cori had something important, something maybe no one else on the planet had:

information on a single population of frogs from *before* and *after* the killer came knocking.

Cori focused her attention on one question: what was different about the frogs after the disease hit?

Somewhere, inside all those numbers, she just knew there had to be clues. She sifted and sorted the info. She plotted and processed the numbers. Then she spotted a pattern: after the infection, the frogs she found had higher body temperatures than before the pandemic.

Cori's next step was to dig in and discover what others had already discovered. She was reading about infections and reading about frogs and reading about animal temperatures when one story jumped out at her. A plague of locusts was munching its way through farmers' crops. Researchers had tried to help by spraying a fungus that would kill the crop-crunching critters.

Locusts are relatives of grasshoppers. A single swarm can contain 80 million locusts!

But the locusts had climbed up the plant stalks, basked in the sun, and fought off the fungus.

Those insects used heat from the sun to give themselves a fever. The fever helped them kill the fungus.

Cori wondered: Could the golden frogs be doing something similar?

Bradley Bd grows best from 63 to 77°F. When temps rise to 82°, the fungus stops growing. At 86°, chytrid kicks the bucket. So a hot body could be a good way to kill off this bad guy.

Fish do it. Researchers have discovered that if you give an infected guppy a choice:

Tank #1 at 57°F

Tank #2 at 65°F

Tank #3 at 90°F

. . . he'll hang out in the warmest water. (Uninfected guppies choose chillier water.) After three days in the hot tub, the parasites perish. When a desert iguana needs to beat a bacterium, she slips out of the shadows and cranks up the heat. And when your body faces an infection, it makes use of that hot little trick, too.

FUN FACT

Mitochondria produce 90 percent of the energy you use. Almost every cell in your body has several thousand of them.

Heat from inside an animal comes from mitochondria. Mitochondria convert sugar into energy. Without those powerhouses, we'd have no energy—and no heat. A human brain regulates that heat to maintain a steady temperature all over the body, except for when it needs a fever to fight a pathogen. Iguanas, guppies, locusts, and frogs are a bit different from humans—instead of regulating their own body temperature, they rely on heat from the air, the water, the sun—so, if they want to spike a fever, they bask in the sun to bring their temperature up.

Don't say "cold-blooded"—on a sunny rock in July, their blood would be blazing hot. Get your science speak on and call them "ectotherms." **ECTO** = outside; **THERM** = temperature.

Other researchers have found that frogs who live in hot springs can survive chytrid. Still others discovered that frogs who live lower on the mountain (where temperatures are warmer) may survive when their neighbors just up the chilly hill don't.

Soon, Cori had a hypothesis: body temperature affects fungal infection. Was it true that the warmer the frog, the lower the incidence of infection?

Were Panamanian golden frogs giving themselves a fever to fight the fungus?

HI-YAH! Take that, you freaky fungus!

Not so fast.

Cori was seeing a relationship—a connection called a correlation—between temperature and infection. But every good scientist knows that correlation is not the same as causation. In other words, although Cori noticed a *connection* between frogs' body temperature and their survival, there wasn't enough evidence to say that warm temperatures *caused* the fungus to die or that the frogs *intentionally* warmed up.

Now what? Cori couldn't go asking, "Hey, Golden Girl, are you lucky and just happened to be in a warm spot, or are you a genius who knew you needed a temp to foil the fungus?"

Our determined scientist set up a test. In a lab, she used heating coils and an aquarium chiller to create channels that were hot on one end and cold on the other.

Welcome to your new home, little froggies!

Healthy golden frogs chose to hang out at about 68°F. Next, Cori gave them a bath—but instead of bubbles in their tub, they got 50,000 bodacious zoospores!

When they went back into their hot/cold home, would they hip-hop over to the warm side? Would they cure themselves of the chytrid curse?

It sure would be convenient if they had. Instead, the frogs stuck to their own favorite spots. Pick one up and put it in the center, and he'd hop back to his original spot as if to say, "I'm fine right here, thank you very much."

HMMM.

Cori could have gotten frustrated. She could have gotten stuck on her earlier idea, but instead, she kept looking. She peeked under the frogs' skin to see how the fungus was doing.

And that's when Cori spotted another pattern—a pattern that was the opposite of what she expected:

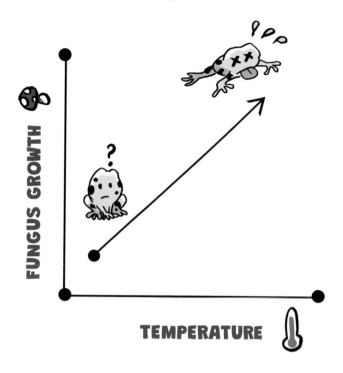

The warmer the frog, the faster the fungus was growing. What?!

Was her fever idea totally wrong?

MAYBE.

Or maybe not.

Cori posed another possibility: maybe individual Flavio Frogs have temperatures they prefer. That could explain what she had observed out in the wilds of Panama. There, frogs who preferred cooler temps might have died from chytrid, leaving behind a population of heat-loving frogs.

In an experiment, there can be many reasons for unexpected results. When Cori tested other species in the same way, they *had* hopped on over to the heated end. And in some frogs, the fungus numbers did drop as their temperature warmed up.

The truth is, science isn't "one and done." One scientific study doesn't give us an answer—it gives us a piece of the puzzle.

But one piece of the puzzle was not enough to satisfy Cori . . .

IDEAS EVOLVE

The Panamanian golden frog has a sister species called the variable harlequin frog that was also affected by chytrid. After the epidemic, sightings of the harlequins had become so rare people assumed they were extinct.

Then, in 2012, a harlequin frog was found!

Suddenly, Cori and her colleagues had hope: Could the population of harlequin frogs bounce back? Were other species surviving in the shadows? To answer their questions, these amphibian allies took off to Panama on a new quest: would they find more frogs?

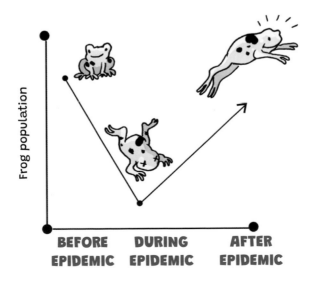

Frog population

BEFORE EPIDEMIC   DURING EPIDEMIC   AFTER EPIDEMIC

GOOD NEWS!

Some populations of some species were starting to recover. Yet, the fungus had not disappeared. The fungus is still among us. How had those hip-hoppers managed to survive?

Cori had a hunch about a slimy weapon—mucus!

Like the mucus in your nose, frog mucus contains AMPs. AMP stands for **anti**M**icrobial **p**eptide. A peptide is a small protein. These particular ones fight against (anti) microscopic pathogens (microbes). In other words, AMPs are like miniature bullets aimed at teeny-tiny bad guys.

A few of Cori's frog-loving friends, Jamie Voyles, Doug Woodhams, and Louise Rollins-Smith, had sucked up some frog slime from before the pandemic. Comparing that slime to slime from after the fungus hit, they found the survivors' slime had more-potent AMPs.

Why were survivors able to make more-powerful proteins? Perhaps what these scientists were seeing was natural selection at work.

Each frog's AMPs are determined by its DNA. If frogs who carried DNA for stronger AMPs survived, they could live to become mama and papa peepers. They could pass that successful DNA recipe on to their tadpoles, and the population would evolve.

NATURAL SELECTION = only the best survive what nature throws at them.

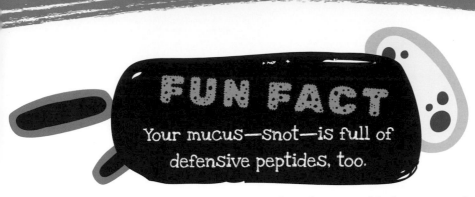

The frog slime was a strong clue, but would the researchers' idea about natural selection hold up if they dug into the DNA? Cori pulled out those frog toes she had collected long, long ago. That DNA was from before the pandemic. When Cori and her biologist buddy Allie Byrne compared the genes from before and after, they found that, sure enough, some of the genes to make powerful proteins were more prevalent in the frogs who survived.

Cori's new hypothesis: maybe superior slime matters more than temperature in the fight against the fungus. If that is true, the pandemic could be speeding up natural selection by weeding out the frogs with the weakest genes. In other words, the infection could be making future generations stronger!

Is that happening in this frog population? Cori needs more evidence before she can draw that conclusion. So, she's collecting more clues, seeking more patterns, keeping her mind open to allow her ideas to evolve.

In the cloud forest of Panama, some frogs may have a secret, slimy weapon.

NOT·SO·FUN FACT

Sadly, the Panamanian golden frog is still critically endangered. As long as populations are kept alive in captivity, though, there's still hope!

CHAPTER 3

Awesome Ant Adaptations

FUN FACT

When lobsters, monkeys, ants, or bullfrog tadpoles are sick, their pals can sniff the sick.

In a plastic petri dish, three black ants swarm over one white ant body.

Crunch. Black mouthparts mash together.

Plop! A white leg falls to the ground.

The scientist leans in. What? Why are black ants biting the legs off a white ant? Even odder: This is no war between enemy ant colonies; these are grown-ups gnawing on a kid. (Not a human kid—a kid from their own colony!)

The adults are tearing into a pupa.

> ANT LIFE CYCLE =
> Egg ➡ larva ➡ pupa ➡ adult.
> PUPA = the stage where the cocooned critter looks like it's taking a nap.

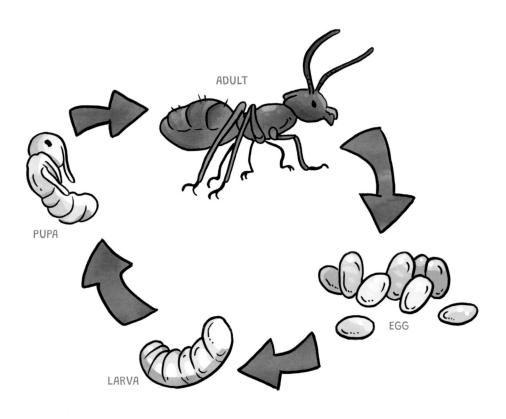

ADULT

PUPA

EGG

LARVA

POP! The mouthparts of the adult ants punch like fists.

They stab like short swords.

They leave gaping gashes in the pupa's side.

She lies helpless.

Goo drips from her guts.

Why were these ants killing their own kin?

Well, that white ant wasn't any old regular pupa. She (and a few of her sisters) had been given a gift. But it wasn't the kind of gift you'd wish on any of your friends. It was a thousand or so spores—eensy-teensy packages of pathogen. Spores of the fungus *Metarhizium brunneum*. We'll use Meta for short.

NOT-SO-FUN FACT

The fungus *Metarhizium brunneum* can kill over 200 kinds of insects.

These spores had been handed out by a scientist—Christopher Pull. Why did Christopher give such a ghastly gift? Was he some kind of maniacal meanie? Nope, Christopher (and an entire team of scientists) had sacrificed that pupa because he was keen to know: how can an ant colony kick out a fungus?

FUNGUS AMONG US

If you were a parasitic fungus, your perfect paradise might be a deep, dark dungeon of dirt. And if you were Meta, you'd love nothing more than to weasel your way into a garden ant nest and pig out on some six-legged supper!

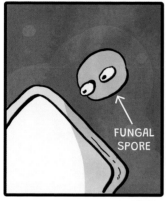

FUNGAL SPORE

LEVEL 1 QUEST: Seek and destroy Ant #543

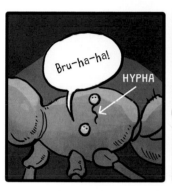

Bru-ha-ha!

HYPHA

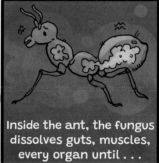

Inside the ant, the fungus dissolves guts, muscles, every organ until . . .

LEVEL 2 QUEST: Conquer colony

CRICK! CRACK!

POOF!

When the fluff turns the color of vomit, sticky spores are ready to spread.

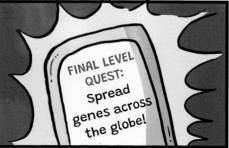

FINAL LEVEL QUEST: Spread genes across the globe!

But we're talking about ants, super ants, super insects that work together as a super organism. Ants know how to deal with ferocious fungi. They've got guards. They've got stations. They've got adaptations!

Here's an Ant Super Strategy: stop the spores before they get started.

When Aiysha Ant comes home from foraging, Ada Ant (a sanitary worker) puts her mouth mandibles to work, grooming off the grit. How would you like to lick 100 sisters clean every night?

PINCH AND PLUCK.

Ada works her mandibles like tweezers. Now, how's a gal supposed to hold a bazillion balls of bad and keep them from spilling all over the nest? No trash can, no toilet, no pants pocket to tuck them into. What can she do?

POP!

She shoves them into her mouth. Into her mouth pocket. Yep, a pocket inside her mouth.

Told you she had adaptations!

FUN FACT

Although mouth pockets were discovered a century ago, humans are just now learning of their many uses. What would you use one for?

Wait, won't the spores just germinate in Ada?

Give an ant some credit!

Ada leans down—way, way down—till her mouth stops beside her rear end.

Lick, lick. That should do the trick.

From a petite pore, Ada slurps venom. It's not one, but two acids swirled together to create Double-Strength Annihilating Acid!

Ada doesn't swallow the stuff. She swishes it into her mouth pocket to sanitize those spores.

PTUI! She spits the sanitized spores into the trash heap. Talk about awesome adaptations.

NOT-SO-FUN FACT

Stick your nose in the bed of some ants, and they'll shoot acid into your eye!

For millions of years, ants have been evading fungal fiends.

But for millions of years, this fungus has been fighting back. Sometimes, a super-sticky spore sneaks past the sanitizers. A single spore invading a single ant can turn into millions more, meaning . . .

That could kill the colony.

Yet, somehow, ants live on . . .

SPYING ON SPORES

Christopher Pull and a whole team of experts want to know: what happens when the first line of ant defenses fails and the spores invade the most precious parts of the nest—the places reserved for the queen or the kids?

And *that* is why Christopher had splashed fungal spores onto some pupae. His teammates had already seen that when pupae become infected, the nursery workers whisk them away from all the other pupae. Smart move. But what happened next?

You can't whip out a microphone to interview ants. So

Christopher whipped out the *microscope* to *watch* the ants.

GRAB.
JERK.
TWIST.

RIP!

The ant is spraying acid!

Christopher's question: Couldn't they simply squirt the pupal case?

?

And then Christopher started experimenting.

Time to test . . .

SPRITZ-SPRITZ!

ANT ACID

The pupal case repels acid!

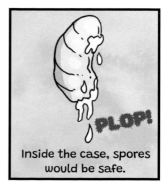

PLOP!

Inside the case, spores would be safe.

Then Christopher watched some more.

Limb by limb, the workers
chop the pupa to pieces—

Christopher's question:
Why do they kill the kid?

And then he experimented some more.

The only way to find out was . . .

. . . to kill some kids himself!

Don't get the wrong idea. Christopher didn't *want* to kill the ants. He is an animal lover. When he was a kid, his bedroom was a zoo: chameleons, scorpions, and stick insects everywhere.

But Christopher had to get to the bottom of this mystery. To understand if each of those steps was important, he set up three studies:

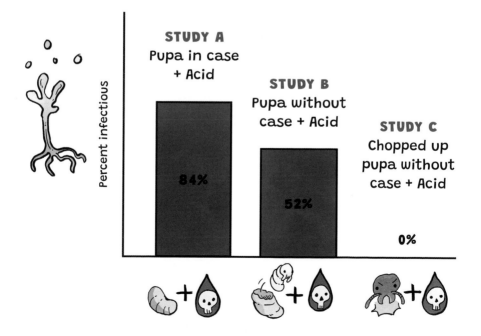

It took all three steps to stop the spreading. If the adults don't remove the case, the spores hide inside it. If they don't stab through the exoskeleton, the spores hide inside *that*.

One infectious pupa can infect 40 percent of the colony, so if the nursery workers let spores germinate in even a single pupa . . .

Thankfully the ants have evolved this powerful system. They sacrifice a few lives to save lots of lives.

PEOPLE PARALLEL

Why were Christopher and this crew so committed to ants and their battle with a fungus? Because when they looked at the way ants protect their colonies, they noticed similarities to how people protect their bodies:

BATTLE READY!

ANT NEST

Walls stand strong

Soldiers are ready
to defend at every
opening

Sanitary ants suck
in scum

Nursery workers kill
infected kids

HUMAN BODY

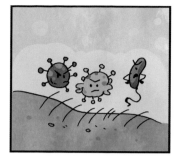

Skin stands strong

Mucus and microbes,
acid and enzymes
defend at every opening

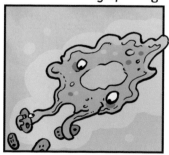

Macrophages suck
in intruders

Natural killer cells
kill infected cells

BLOCK!

GUARD!

EXTERMINATE!

SACRIFICE!

The team saw similarities between the ants and the cells in human innate immune systems.

Meet your innate immune system— super-fast, super-strong, it's the body's first line of defense!

The innate system has an entire infantry of white blood cells designed for instant annihilation of the enemy. Like guard ants patrolling underground tunnels, your cell soldiers cruise your body, seeking intruders.

INNATE = already present at birth.

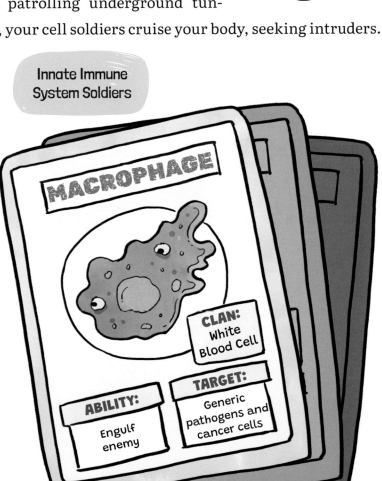

Innate Immune System Soldiers

MACROPHAGE

CLAN: White Blood Cell

ABILITY: Engulf enemy

TARGET: Generic pathogens and cancer cells

NATURAL KILLER CELL

CLAN:
White Blood Cell

ABILITY:
Punch holes in enemies' membranes

TARGET:
Tumors and virus-infected cells

NEUTROPHIL

CLAN:
White Blood Cell

ABILITY:
Spew toxin, cast nets, mobilize backups

TARGET:
Bacteria and fungi!

DEND

Ants seem like such simple beings, but those eensy-teensy six-leggers have awesome adaptations. And they have lots to teach us. Sure, we can learn fun facts (mouth pockets!), but we can also learn strategies (using acid to annihilate pathogens). Even more importantly, if we step back to get the big picture, we can learn by analogy (ant colonies compared to human bodies).

Human immune systems are complex—like 1,000 puzzles mixed together. All those puzzle pieces are microscopic and hidden inside living people. Kind of hard to put our eyeballs on them . . . But with ant colonies, we can *see* the workers. We can *watch* the ants trek in and out of the nest. We can *recognize* that Ada and Aiysha and all their sisters give us a model to better understand ourselves.

FUN FACT

Worker garden ants who are exposed to small doses of spores are healthier than those who are never exposed. It's ant vaccination!

Gator Aid

A dark tail swishes. A wet head rises. A gray snout splits into two toothy jaws.

SNAP! The alligator's teeth chomp down on something sitting at the edge of the shore. Adam Alligator's not biting for breakfast. He's not lunging for lunch. His jaws have clamped on to the leg of Gilbert Gator. A guy gator can't tolerate another male moving into his territory. Adam's got to defend his sunning spot, his hunting ground, his chance to get a girl.

Tails slap, legs flail, one white belly spins toward the sky. Then, Adam eases back into the swamp, with his prize hanging from his jaws.

Gilbert's left standing, awkwardly, balancing on just three paws . . .

Mark Merchant has been mucking around in marsh mud for years. He's seen over 100 alligators with body parts missing. Mark wondered: how are they still alive?

Never mind the blood they lost. Never mind how hard it would be to hunt when you are one leg down. What Mark needed to know was: how could a wound swish through all that swampy water and not rot?

Remember, skin is the body's fortress wall. Sure, pathogens can wiggle their way into official openings—up the nose, down the throat—and there are baddies like Bradley Bd who can break in through skin, but, mostly, skin keeps the ick out. When skin gets slit wide, though, it lets good stuff out and dangerous stuff in. It's an open invitation to all those outsiders.

Gator habitats are not exactly clean. Swamps, ditches, marshes. On top of the normal mud, in some places, wetlands are also swirling with sewage. Imagine dipping your leg in a dirty toilet. Imagine dangling an open wound in there for days . . .

BACTERIAL BASICS

One thing you'll find stewing and brewing in swampy water: those single-celled organisms we call bacteria. There's no shortage of bacterial bad guys on our planet. Pathogenic bacteria can cause diseases like tuberculosis, pneumonia, and the plague.

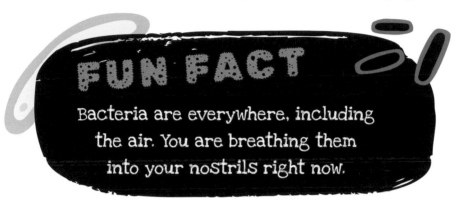

FUN FACT

Bacteria are everywhere, including the air. You are breathing them into your nostrils right now.

Then there are the flesh eaters. In humans, those daredevils can calmly cause bad breath or gum disease, or they can slip into the blood, slide up to the skull, then scrape out a pus-filled pocket in the brain.

FORTUNATE FACT

Serious infections of flesh-eating fusobacterium are rare. For example, over an 11-year period, out of 1.3 million people surveyed, only 72 cases of fusobacterium were found—and they weren't all that bad.

You've probably forgotten to wash out a wound. In a few days, you're given a gift: puffy, pussy pain. Thanks, bacteria!

On the other hand, bacteria can be good guys. Researchers go gaga over what bacteria can give us: new medicines, new species, new ways of looking at the world—bacteria can do that. In fact, every animal alive should thank bacteria. Soil bacteria pull nitrogen from the air and convert it into a form that plants can use. Without that, there'd be no fertilizer. No fertilizer, no plants. No plants, no food.

If a gator chomped your leg off, what beautiful bacteria might decide to inhabit the wound? Let's say one of these bacteria is *Staphylococcus aureus*, a bacterium named for its grape shape. *Staphyle* means "grape," and *kokkos* means "berries."

Peer into a lab dish full of happy staph, and you'll see bunches of yellow colonies. Peer into a microscope, and you'll see that each colony is a cluster of innocent-looking balls. But peer into infected skin, and you'll see a red-hot, nasty wound. Yellow may be spilling out of it, but that won't be staph leaving your body. That will be pus—your own immune warriors who are now dead and oozing off the battlefield.

Okay, maybe there will be a few dead staph cells in there, too, but Stephanie Staph is a vicious opponent who can colonize quickly. When conditions are right, a single staph cell can duplicate itself every half hour. Unlike animals, bacteria can copy *themselves*. Over and over and over until there's a whole colony of clones. In less than 12 hours, more than a million identical staph cells could be kickin' it in your body.

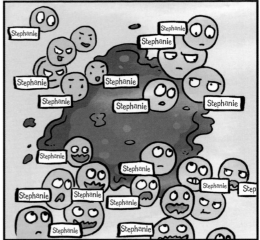

Don't worry. When staph invades the fortress of your skin, your innate immune system springs into action. Hmmm. That sounds suspiciously like what happens when someone hacks a hole in an ant nest. Special proteins called complement proteins start marking the bacteria—

—and label those cells as intruders.

First responders like mast cells and dendritic cells get to work, but the bacteria keep coming. The colonies keep cloning. Soon, it's more than those first responders can handle.

So they send messages—in the form of signal molecules—to the rest of the team.

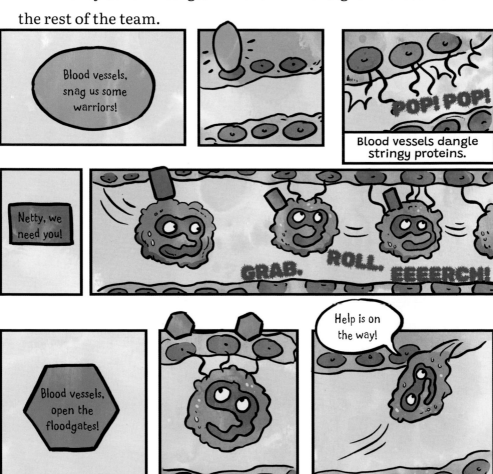

Now **THIS** is inflammation in action! Every player is flooding into the area, working together to do a job and to rid the body of unwanted intruders. Here's a star of the innate immune system: Netty Neutrophil.

The tag triggers Netty to launch one of three strategies:

Battle Strategy #1:

Battle Strategy #2:

Battle Strategy #3:

In your body, within minutes of a bacterium invading your skin, your awesome immune system could do all of that. Except Stephanie doesn't always surrender so simply.

SUPERIOR STAPH

Staph has been infecting human beings for at least 10,000 years and has figured out a few ways to fight back.

In a single year, *Staphylococcus aureus* caused 119,000 serious infections in Americans and killed 20,000 people. One strain of staph, called MRSA, has become especially deadly. In some situations, it can kill up to 60 percent of infected patients. That's 6 out of every 10. That strain has even learned how to evade antibiotic medicines. That's pretty creepy!

Where is MRSA most common? Hospitals, doctors' offices, and other health-care settings—the very places you would expect to be germ-free! The good news: keeping your hands clean is an easy way to beat this superbug.

Stephanie Staph is a pro at evading human immune systems. Peek in on an infection and you'll witness teeny-tiny bacteria outwitting Netty Neutrophil at every turn:

1

Bombs disarmed by staph's yellow pigment

2

Receptors blocked by staph's toxin

3

Nets smashed by staph's enzymes

And that's just the neutrophils *and* just the innate immune system. Staph also shuts down the signaling molecules that are *supposed* to recruit more help, releases toxins to harm the cells that are *supposed* to bulldoze bacteria, and cuts off the signals that are *supposed* to turn on the acquired immune system!

No wonder people are dying.

ACQUIRED = not present at birth. The acquired immune system develops with every exposure to pathogens. It's also called the "adaptive" immune system since it *adapts* to the pathogens it encounters.

GATOR MAGIC

But gators like Gilbert are surviving. See why Mark was surprised?

Mark is a biochemist: he's fascinated by molecules, their shapes, and how they function inside animal bodies. Mark wondered if gator blood carried unique molecules to beat out the bacteria. One day, his boss challenged him to follow his questions. So, Mark headed to the water, wrestled some gators, and went after answers.

PRICK. SLIP. SUCTION.

With a needle-tipped syringe, Mark extracted vials of rich red blood from alligator necks. Then he let the blood sit. When he came back later, gravity had done its job. At the bottom of the vial sat dark red matter. The heavy red blood cells had settled there. At the top of the vial floated clear yellow liquid. That was plasma, mostly water. Right in the middle was a thin, cream-colored layer—the white blood cells where immune action happens!

Each vial held only a smidge of those cells, so he carefully sucked them up (with a clean syringe, not his mouth!). He used a centrifuge machine to spin the cells in circles and shake them down into a tiny pellet.

Next, he had a challenge. How could he discover what the microscopic cells were capable of?

First, Mark needed bacteria for his gator blood to battle.

Sixteen different bacteria, all gobbled by gator blood!

Obviously, the gator blood cells wielded power. In one test they killed 10 times more bacteria than human cells did.

They were fast, too. Within 5 minutes, they had obliterated thousands of bacterial bodies.

These cells were amazing, but they were a mystery to Mark. So, he went searching for info. In books, in magazines, in computer databases . . . nothing. Had no one studied alligators' awesome immune systems? Had no one realized that gators could be holding secrets to survival? Had no one wondered if gator blood could help humans?

Mark did. What if gator blood *did* contain some miracle molecule? What if he could make medicine from it to save human lives?

FUN FACT

Along with gharials and crocodiles, alligators belong to the scientific order called Crocodilia, a group of toothy beasts who have been on the planet since before dinosaurs existed.

Twenty years ago, Mark grabbed ahold of those questions and never looked back. Ever since, he's been hopping the globe, wrangling gators, crocs, caimans, and more to decipher their chemical clues.

He found that all that killing power came from a teeny-tiny protein, an antimicrobial peptide. Remember the frog slime packed with fungus-fighting AMPs? It's the same kind of protein, only gator-powered!

The power of an AMP comes from strong positive charges. The membranes of its foe, the bacteria, have negative charges. Like a bit of metal near a magnet, the AMP is drawn to the bigger bacteria.

Once the AMP binds to the bacteria—

And just like with your skin, once there are holes in a bacterium's cell wall—

dangerous stuff
can go in . . .

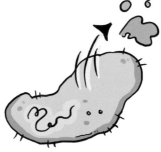

. . . and good stuff
can go out.

Bye-bye, bacteria!

THE RACE IS ON

People have AMPs, too. Compared to gator AMP champs, though, human AMPs are wimps.

Alligator AMPs can also burst the bacteria that cause strep throat and pneumonia. Hey, they don't stop at bacteria. They chew through the tough membranes of fungi. They can even put a halt to viruses like HIV (the virus that causes AIDS in humans).

Think of how strong AMPs give animals a leg up against germs. When an adaptation (like stronger frog slime) makes an individual immune to a germ, then that animal's young may inherit the adaptation and survive, too. Good old "survival of the fittest." That's one way animal species evolve through time.

But germs are in that "survival of the fittest" race, too. If a germ happens to have an adaptation that lets it overcome the animal's most recent adaptation, then it will survive. It will reproduce. It will evolve, too.

The race is on!

Back and forth they go. Say a mutation gives the animal stronger skin, then most germs can't even get in. Those germs die

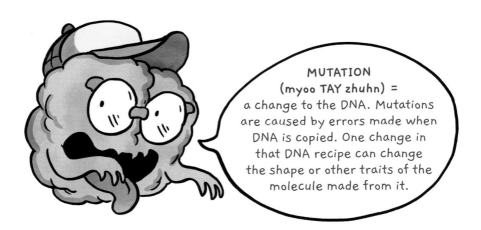

MUTATION
(myoo TAY zhuhn) =
a change to the DNA. Mutations
are caused by errors made when
DNA is copied. One change in
that DNA recipe can change
the shape or other traits of the
molecule made from it.

off. The animal surges ahead in the race. But that puts pressure—natural selection pressure—on the germ. If any germ happens to carry a mutation that gives it an advantage, *that* germ will thrive and reproduce . . .

Evolution in action!

The race goes on and on, each organism's adaptations egging on the other organism.

In the race against bacteria, alligators seem to be miles ahead. It's as if their AMPs created a roadblock the pathogens can't get around. Because those AMPs punch holes directly into cell walls, it is hard for pathogens to develop resistance to them.

How have gator bodies figured out tricks ours haven't? Why are gator AMPs stronger than all our medicines?

Maybe because alligators are old, like before-dinosaurs old. Their kind has been battling bacteria for the past 200 million years. They've seen a few epidemics. And with every epidemic, their immune systems got stronger and smarter.

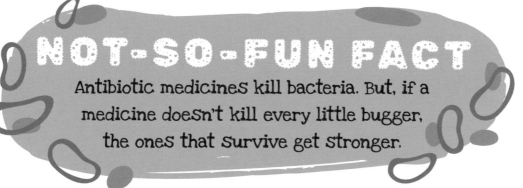

NOT-SO-FUN FACT

Antibiotic medicines kill bacteria. But, if a medicine doesn't kill every little bugger, the ones that survive get stronger.

CHAPTER 5
Buzzard Buddies?

Gary Graves put on his gown, goggles, and gloves. He grabbed syringes and swabs. He spent a week collecting DNA samples from the outside and the inside of 24 vulture carcasses.

> Carcass = a dead body.

First—

DAB, DAB—

he gathered goo from their faces.

Second—

SNIP, SLICE, STRETCH—

he opened the bird bellies and pulled out 5 feet of guts.

Third—

STAB, SQUISH, SUCK—

He squirted liquid in with a syringe, he mushed and squished it inside the gut, and then he sucked it back out. That backwash is what Gary was after.

Gary was searching for bacteria on or in vulture bodies to answer one burning question: why don't vultures get sick?

FUN FACT
A group of vultures can be called a volt, venue, committee, colony, or kettle.

Vultures tromp through the rotten, plunge their tongues into the putrid, and gulp down the gross. If *you* ate what *they* ate, you would vomit volumes. Your innards might explode. You might die from diarrhea. Because what Victor Vulture eats is a whole lot of rot—rot caused by bacteria.

Any old bacteria, like salmonella, can put a hurtin' on regular old birds like house finches and sparrows, or heroic birds like herons and hawks. But a vulture? Nope. Gary had studied birds for 50 years. Did he know of *any* bacterial diseases in vultures? Nope. None. For years people have been making guesses about how vultures avoid pathogenic bacteria:

GUESS #1:
They drip their waste down to their toes to destroy diseases.

GUESS #2:
Their noggin is nude so no stinky stuff sticks.

GUESS #3:
They gulp the dead down before it gets gross.

FUN FACT

Vulture stomachs are as acidic as vinegar. And yours is, too.

But those are just guesses. Is there any evidence? Five researchers (Barbara, Daniel, Fabrine, Tiana, and Tiandra) set out to investigate.

Their quest: to understand how death eaters avoid illness.

Their method: crank up the computer, click into the Web of Science database, begin myth-busting!

GUESS #1: To pee and poop, vultures have only one opening, so the pee and poop mix together and come out as greasy white slop. It *does* slide down the vultures' shins, but the researchers found no formal studies indicating the plop had germ–killing capacity.

GUESS #2: Turkey vultures are known for their featherless red heads. Could this help them keep germy goop off their faces? Not as far as the scientists could tell. Instead, vulture heads may be bare to keep their brains cool.

GUESS #3: Maybe vultures swallow before bacteria have time to grow? Fact hounds found no evidence for that idea either!

FUN FACT

Vultures need help cutting bodies open. If no other animal steps up with a slicing beak or jabbing jaw, a vulture will poke and prod their way in through the easiest opening—the one at the animal's rear end!

New World vultures (turkey vultures, black vultures, American condors, etc.) live in the Americas.

Old World vultures (bearded vultures, griffon vultures, white-rumped vultures, etc.) live in Africa, Asia, and Europe. Though they act like close cousins, these groups are barely related.

If purifying pee, nude noggins, and ghastly gulps aren't saving vultures from sickness, what is?

To figure that out, we first need to get to know a bacterium named clostridium.

FUN FACT

Vultures sun their wings, creating an extremely harsh habitat: intense heat, UV radiation, and no water. Perfect for *Deinococcus*, a berry-shaped bacteria so tough some scientists wonder if it originally came from outer space.

CLOSTRIDIA CLAN

Say you swallowed some stew that was not cooked completely, then ten hours later your stomach was swirling as if it had set sail in a storm. Or perhaps you tucked into turkey that sat on the counter too long. Later, your tummy felt crummy, and you spent all night squatting and squirting.

Meet Presley Perfringens, scientifically known as *Clostridium perfringens*. There are more than 200 types of clostridia, but Presley is particularly pesky and responsible for nearly one million cases of diarrhea a year—and that's only in the US—and that's only in two-leggeds.

Presley and his perfringens crew have a whole slew of toxins that play in animal intestines:

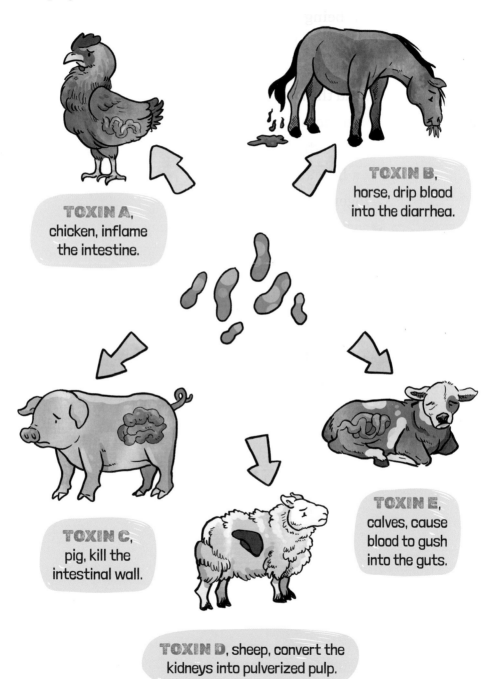

TOXIN A, chicken, inflame the intestine.

TOXIN B, horse, drip blood into the diarrhea.

TOXIN C, pig, kill the intestinal wall.

TOXIN D, sheep, convert the kidneys into pulverized pulp.

TOXIN E, calves, cause blood to gush into the guts.

That's just a small sample of symptoms. Clostridia can also cause death in chinchillas and children.

If, instead of being swallowed, Presley goes in through the skin, he provides a whole different suite of treats: blisters that boil purple plus gross gas under the skin, which can require a surgeon, a scalpel, and the loss of a limb.

Terrible toxins doing dastardly deeds.

By himself, though, Presley doesn't have the power to kill a pig, sheep, *and* a human. To do that, he would need the help of Priscilla Perfringens, Pierre Perfringens, Paul Perfringens . . . Every C. *perfringens* carries a different concoction of toxin, which might not seem so odd until you remember that bacteria often are clones of one another. Until you think about how their genetic code should be exactly equal. Until you realize it would be like triplet snake sisters, each one with venom to kill only a mouse or a bunny or a lizard. In snakes and every other *normal* animal, adaptations like venom don't vary so drastically because they get passed down in the family recipe, the genetic code.

P.S. Bacteria are not normal.

P.P.S. Bacteria aren't animals.

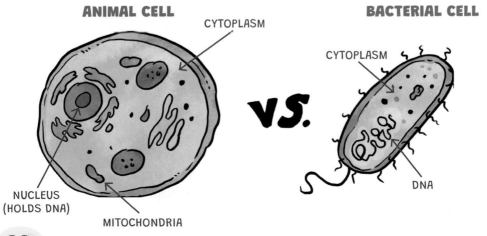

ANIMAL CELL

CYTOPLASM

VS.

BACTERIAL CELL

CYTOPLASM

DNA

NUCLEUS
(HOLDS DNA)

MITOCHONDRIA

Bacteria cells are simple. They have no organelles. No mitochondria to produce energy. No nucleus to keep DNA safe. The precious genetic code from Presley's ancestors sits in a jumble in the cellular soup called cytoplasm.

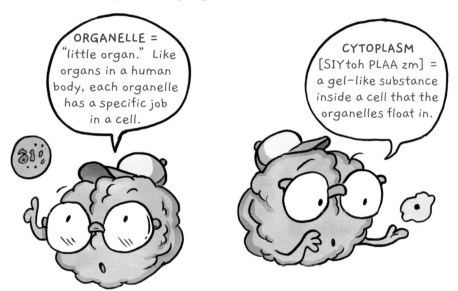

ORGANELLE = "little organ." Like organs in a human body, each organelle has a specific job in a cell.

CYTOPLASM [SIYtoh PLAA zm] = a gel-like substance inside a cell that the organelles float in.

Unlike animals, bacteria don't just have DNA inherited from their ancestors. They have extra little loops of DNA called plasmids. Plasmid DNA can hold instructions that give bacteria superpowers like surviving poison, killing other bacteria, or munching on pollution. And plasmids can contain recipes for making a variety of toxins.

Baby bacteria *can* get plasmids from their parent, but they can also *take* toxin-creating plasmids from other bacteria!

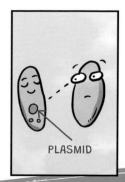
PLASMID

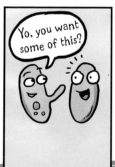
Yo, you want some of this?

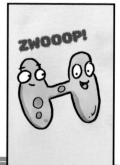
ZWOOOP!

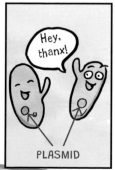
Hey, thanx!
PLASMID

And that little trick allows Presley Perfringens and Priscilla Perfringens and Pierre Perfringens each to create different toxic cocktails—perfect for tricking immune warriors from all kinds of animals.

FUN FACT

Some plasmids hold a bacterium hostage by producing a long-lasting toxin and a short-term antidote. Surely the bacterium doesn't like the toxin, but it must keep the plasmid around to keep getting doses of antidote.

Victor Vulture must get exposed to clostridia all the time. For sure there's some on his supper, but also, every time he wades into the crowd at the buzzard buffet, he rubs shoulders with bacteria-covered buds. Even at bedtime he can't escape. If the guy on the limb upstairs needs to take a leak, plip-plop, Vic gets a splatter! In a vulture's life, it's bacteria here, bacteria there, bacteria everywhere.

Maybe, like chimps, vultures take advantage of treetop pharmacies? Nope. Well, not that we know of.

Maybe all birds get a free pass from sick symptoms? Nope. In 1982, 1,500 ducks died from dining on clostridium-infected flies. In a separate epidemic, a different kind of clostridium killed 8,000 ring-necked pheasants.

Then why aren't buzzards keeled over on the curb? Why aren't vet clinics filled with vomiting vultures? Can you see why Gary's mind kept swirling around that unanswered question: why don't vultures get sick!?

In the US, folks gave vultures the nickname "buzzards." In the rest of the world, BUZZARD = hawk.

And, as they usually do, one question morphed into more questions:

What makes them immune?

Why are they immune?

How are they immune?

Could we learn some of their tricks?

And that's why Gary was dabbing, stabbing, and sucking bacteria off our feathered friends. He was building a list of buzzard bacteria.

He could have started by peeking in their poo. One problem with that: a pile of poo isn't pure. Every grain of dirt and every dot of dust is coated with bacteria. To get "clean" gunk, he needed access to the internal scene—he needed a bunch of fresh buzzard guts.

Every year, 3,000 to 4,000 vultures are killed by the US Department of Agriculture. They're not doing it for fun, they're not doing it for food, they're doing it because some citizens think vultures are foul. Sometimes people insist that the government step in to scare, trap, or—as a last resort—kill the birds.

No sense in letting bodies go to waste. Gary swabbed their faces and swished their guts. Then his team separated DNA out of the samples. The DNA of every individual organism is unique, but the DNA of every species has similarities. So, the scientists could match up the DNA they found with code from known species.

It was no surprise: the fowl faces were foul. In addition to DNA from its dinner, each face, on average, was dotted with a wide diversity of bacteria—528 types!

But down in the vultures' guts, the DNA held a few surprises. On average, each bird held DNA from 76 types of bacteria.

528 versus 76.

Where did all that diversity go?

Do vultures clean their beaks? Do they dab away the dirt with a neat napkin? Of course not. How did their bodies avoid getting all that gunk into their guts?

Vultures have a sour stew in their stomachs. Maybe the enzymes and acid destroyed most of the bacteria. Maybe it chopped the stretches of DNA code so small most were beyond recognition.

Gary's syringe-sucking did find recognizable DNA from 76 types of bacteria—evidence that somebody survived the grueling gauntlet of stomach acid.

As Gary was tallying and totaling, he was surprised by something else: which bacteria were dominating the vulture guts.

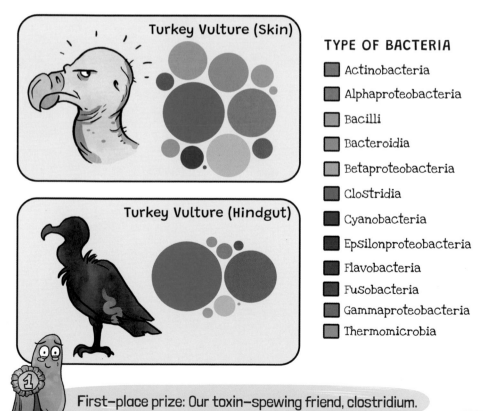

TYPE OF BACTERIA
- Actinobacteria
- Alphaproteobacteria
- Bacilli
- Bacteroidia
- Betaproteobacteria
- Clostridia
- Cyanobacteria
- Epsilonproteobacteria
- Flavobacteria
- Fusobacteria
- Gammaproteobacteria
- Thermomicrobia

First-place prize: Our toxin-spewing friend, clostridium.

How do vultures survive that?

If clostridia are tough enough to make it through stomach acid, tough enough to thrive in a seemingly evil environment, then surely they are tough enough to topple a vulture.

Gary's results raise up a whole slew of other questions: How did those bacteria take over the gut? Were they big bullies who beat out the others, or was there something else at play?

When it comes to understanding vultures and bacteria, Gary's observations aren't the last word—they are more like the first word. Gary doesn't have all the answers, but his results suggest an intriguing idea . . .

If the vultures are thriving *and* the clostridia are thriving, maybe those organisms benefit from living together. The bacteria get a cozy cabin with a steady supply of supper, and the vultures get help digesting dead, disgusting stuff.

Friends?

Friends?

FUN FACT

Scientists have spotted over 1,000 types of microbes (mostly bacteria) in human guts. A single human may host 300 to 500 different types.

One Hump

It was a class *unlike* any other. The students were *not* opening their textbooks. They were *not* following instructions. They were *not* filling in the blanks on worksheets. Because these students were NOT doing the same old, same old boring experiment everyone else had done before.

These students at the Free University of Brussels weren't slackers. Nope. They were embracing a challenge. Normally, to prove they knew how to isolate antibodies from blood, students would demonstrate their skills using human blood. But that procedure had been done a thousand times before, and, the students asked, couldn't they catch a disease from that?

So, their teachers, Raymond Hamers and Cécile Casterman, thought, *How can we shake things up a bit?*

Cécile had the solution: way in the back of their freezer sat a vat of leftover blood. It was from a dromedary camel—the kind with one hump. That should work.

And that is how these students became the first humans to

isolate a mysterious molecule that proved to be an antibody *unlike* any other on the planet.

To truly understand why that discovery made way back in 1989 changed the careers of Cécile and Raymond, why it shocked the world of medical science, and why we still care about it to this very day, you need to meet two key characters: Vera Virion and Anton Antibody.

FUN FACT

Viruses and antibodies are neither male nor female. It's just more fun pretending!

MEET VERA VIRION

SECRET CODE

SPRING-LOADED SPIKES

VIRION (VEER ee uhn) = a complete viral particle in its infectious stage.

EVASIVE ENVELOPE

Unlike some other pathogens, viruses insist on getting intimate. They aren't satisfied with simply slipping under the skin or wandering around in blood vessels. They won't settle for skulking around *between* cells.

NOPE.

A virus slips all the way *inside* an animal's cells . . .

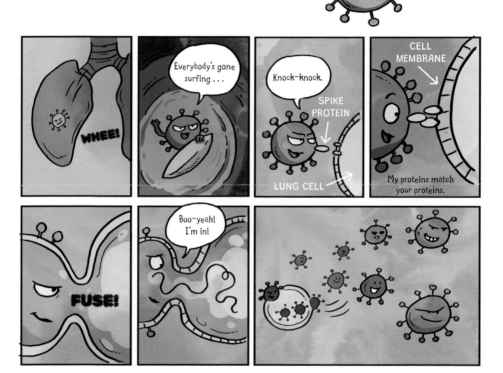

In reality, a virion is pretty helpless by itself. It can't eat, it can't sleep, it can't even make the next generation without the help of a host. A virion doesn't have a nucleus to house its genetic material, a ribosome to make proteins, or even a mitochondrion to provide power. It has to function without the help of any organelles.

To complete its one and only job—making more viruses—a virion like Vera must take over a host's cell, gain control of the cell's machinery, and convert it into a virus-making factory.

Putting the cell to work, a single virion can swiftly become 1,000. And each one of those will go on to infect more of the host's cells until, with some viruses, there are a hundred billion.

That's kinda scary. Fortunately for us mammals, even if a virus slips past the AMPs in our snot, dodges our innate immune warriors, and makes it inside a cell, our bodies have a backup system to shut it down: the acquired immune system, which can annihilate a virus once it gets into a cell.

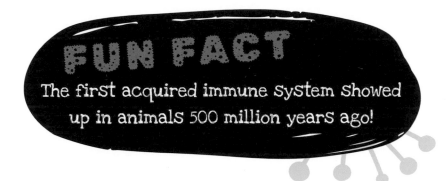

FUN FACT
The first acquired immune system showed up in animals 500 million years ago!

The infected cell sends out a red alert.

Infected.

Infected!

INFECTED!

In rush some of our most elite forces, the natural killer cells and the T cells. What is so special about these warriors? They can force the infected cell to self-destruct.

Just like ant larvae are sacrificed to save the colony, sometimes cells need to be sacrificed to save the rest of the body. But killing off cells isn't a great option. Wouldn't it be better if the virus never got into the cell in the first place? That's one way antibodies can be our heroes.

MEET ANTON THE AVERAGE ANTIBODY

The two tips at the end of an antibody are like puzzle pieces—they fit perfectly with proteins on the envelope of one and only one pathogen.

PATHOGEN GRABBER

HEAVY CHAIN

LIGHT CHAIN

Antibodies play a key role in the acquired immune system. Unlike the innate immune system, which has warriors like Mac the Macrophage and Netty Neutrophil to swiftly conquer any old generic pathogen, the acquired immune system is sort of sluggish. Although it's slower to action, the acquired immune system is specific and smart. And that's a big advantage.

Code name: Immunoglobulin.

Favorite Hangouts: Blood, lymph, spit, snot, breast milk, on the surface of B cells.

Antibodies are made by B cells. Each B cell makes one type of antibody, then coats its own surface with about 100,000 of them. Next, it goes for a trip, cruising the body and using its antibodies to "fish" for its pathogen pair.

FUN FACT

B cells are made by bones. T cells are made by the thymus. The *B* in the B cell name comes from bursa, an organ near the butt of a bird. The function of B cells was first figured out in birds.

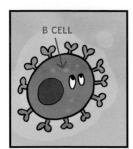

B CELL

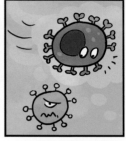

ANTIBODY

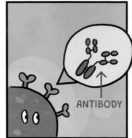

Here fishy, fishy.

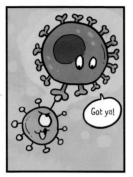

Got ya!

The binding triggers the B cell to clone itself.

A week later . . .

20,000 B cell twins are on the job.

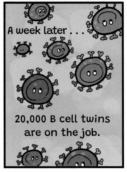

B cells also burp out antibodies— 2,000 per hour!

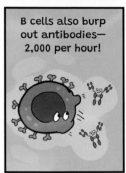

Antibodies can also roam on their own. They can . . .

Grab pathogens and glue them together.

OR

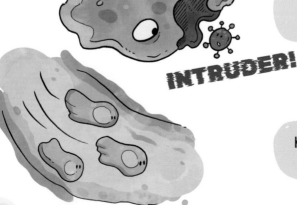

INTRUDER!

Tag toxins for Mac or Netty to destroy.

OR

Kick off inflammation to recruit more help.

Antibodies can wage war against any pathogen that enters the body. But in the war against a virus, their puzzle-piece tips have an extra advantage: they can completely block the virus's ability to enter a cell!

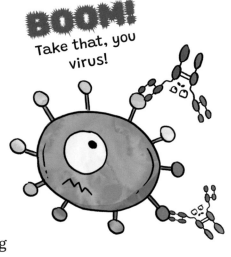

Once the infection is over, most of the B cells fade away, but some hang around. And here's the most amazing thing that Awesome Anton allows the acquired immune system to do: the next time that same virus breaks into the body, those B cells remember its kind and spring into action more quickly. They pump out antibodies so fast, a body might never feel the symptoms.

FUN FACT

A human body can have 3 billion B cells bouncing around in the bloodstream.

Scientists estimate that 1,000 different viruses can cause disease in humans. No problem. Our bodies can make 1,000,000,000,000,000,000 (one quintillion!) different antibodies, each with a unique shape. Take that, you vicious virus!

As you might guess, Vera's got tricks of her own. Viruses know how to sneak past the front lines of defense, how to sidestep our elite forces, and even how to avoid antibodies. When that happens, the body gets sick.

What if an animal body could create an antibody that was smaller, stealthier, and better at snapping on to those villainous viruses?

LABWORK

Remember those students and their mysterious molecule? Let's take a look at how they found it in all that camel blood.

First, they drained away most of the soupy serum from the blood, leaving a sticky glob of molecules. They sat that bloody glob on top of a gel-like material. Then they zapped it all with electricity!

The electrical current made molecules from the blood wiggle through the gel. Smaller molecules can wiggle through smaller spaces, so electricity can pull them faster and farther along the gel. In any old normal blood, there should be whole antibodies plus antibodies split into parts: heavy chains and light chains.

When the students flipped the electricity off, the molecules quit moving. Just as expected, they found whole antibodies and both sizes of parts:

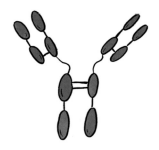

whole antibodies = 150 kDa

heavy chains = 50 kDa

light chains = 25 kDa

kDa = kilodalton, a measure of mass used for weighing atoms, molecules, and other tiny stuff. 1 kilodalton = 1,000 daltons. A hydrogen atom has a mass of 1 dalton.

But they spotted something else, too: molecules with a mass of 90 kDa. What?? No one knew what they could be.

Oh, Cécile and Raymond thought, *the students must have made a mistake.* So, they drew out another sample of camel blood and ran the procedures themselves.

For a second time, the mystery molecules showed up.

Well, they thought, *this blood could be contaminated.* The sample was old; perhaps the molecules had broken down in an unexpected way.

How could they check? Time for a trip to the zoo!

But even in fresh camel blood, the oddball molecule kept popping up. So, the scientists kept checking. Was it in:

- Two-hump camel blood? Yep!
- Any camel cousin's blood? Yep!
- Cow, antelope, human blood? Nope. Nope. Nope.

And that's when Raymond and Cécile started to suspect they were onto something special.

THE MYSTERY MOLECULE IN MODERN TIMES

Today, the mystery molecules are called heavy chain–only antibodies. They are antibodies that don't have light chains. So, they're smaller, savvier, and better at sneaking in and snapping on to pathogens! Let's call them Slim Jims.

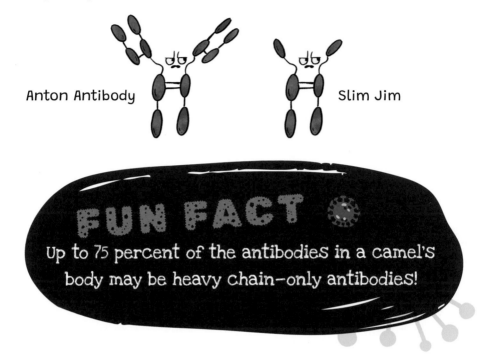

Anton Antibody

Slim Jim

FUN FACT

Up to 75 percent of the antibodies in a camel's body may be heavy chain–only antibodies!

This is super good news for camels and their cousins (llamas, vicuñas, guanacos, and alpacas) who also inherited this mighty mini molecule. Slim Jims seem to have the ability to outsmart viruses in the evolutionary race.

Take a look at how this ancient story might have evolved: Way back in the day, Vera Virion is having her way in an animal. She's slipping past the immune warriors and sliding into cells. She's coaxing the cells to pump out ten, one thousand, one million more virions. What will the fate of our infected animal friend be?

But little does Vera know that one specific antibody has spotted her! And once Anton locks on to those proteins on the envelope, he can activate!

Thanks to Anton, immune warriors can now recognize the virus as an intruder.

There!

There!

THERE!

The animal's body is on the verge of annihilating every last virion. But then . . . Something goes wonky when the virus's genetic code gets copied.

MUTATION!

Normally a mutation leads to a total fail. But sometimes it leads to a variant that can survive. What if Vera's descendants get lucky and that mutated code caused a change in the shape of the envelope proteins—the puzzle pieces the antibodies had been matching up with? Now the protein "looks" different. Suddenly Anton and the other warriors no longer recognize it.

Thanks to this disguise, the virus survives.

Will this spell the end for our furry friend?

Will the virus then spread to the rest of the species?

Wait! What if in that population, there was an animal whose cells also had a mutation? A mutation in the code for their antibodies? Suddenly, that animal's B cells are pumping out antibodies without light chains. And what if that super-slim version has an advantage?

What if it can reach into nooks and crannies where larger antibodies can't? What if it can snap on to parts of the pathogen hidden from other antibodies? What if those sneaky Slim Jims nix the bad guys? That may just be how heavy chain–only antibodies came to be.

Their tiny size gives Slim Jims another grand advantage. On the virus, those standard proteins—the ones Slim Jim can reach right past—are the ones most likely to mutate. When those proteins mutate, that enables a virus to develop a variant, to hide from regular antibodies.

But a variant with mutated proteins doesn't necessarily stop Slim Jims. Because they latch on to different parts of the coat—parts of the virus that are less likely to mutate—Slim Jims are more likely to succeed. Savvy Slim Jim can block the bad guys, even ones who evolve their disguise!

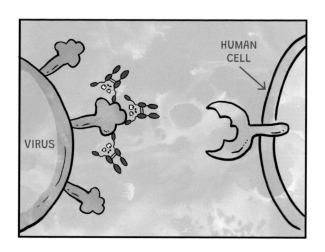

And the reason we now understand the power of camel antibodies? Not a bunch of experts doling out answers. Nope. It was students asking genuine questions. Students who pushed themselves past the same old easy experiment. Students who embraced a challenge, then challenged our understanding of mammal antibodies.

FUN FACT
Sharks also have super-small antibodies that lack light chains.

CHAPTER 7

Bat Bodies

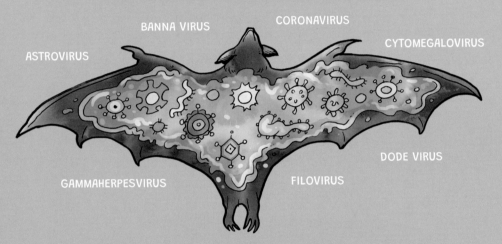

ASTROVIRUS

BANNA VIRUS

CORONAVIRUS

CYTOMEGALOVIRUS

GAMMAHERPESVIRUS

FILOVIRUS

DODE VIRUS

All of those viruses—plus 12,000 more—think bat bodies are bodacious places to live! You would think that would spell disaster for every bat on our planet, yet 1,462 species of bats still flit and flap around.

FUN FACT

Bats live extremely long lives. A Brandt's bat can live 41 years—that's 9.8 times longer than expected of a mouse-sized mammal.

Another odd thing: while a swarm of vicious virus may swirl in her innards, Bailey Bat doesn't even act sick. For years, this lack of symptoms had scientists stumped. Thousands of scientific studies have poked and prodded into the intricacies of bat immune systems, and still, no one completely understands them.

But thanks to Aaron Irving and a team of 16 science sleuths, we now have a clue . . .

Aaron had been studying bats for over 10 years. He loves the way they fly and munch mosquitoes or spread seeds. He values how they pollinate and provide us with fruit—including the world's stinkiest fruit, the durian, which smells like poop! But most urgently, Aaron is curious about how bats can host viruses without showing symptoms.

FUN FACT

Bats pollinate plants by accident. They are actually aiming for the sweet nectar in a flower and get dusted with pollen in the process.

It's the symptoms that make a body feel bad, right? When *your* body is infected by a cold-causing virus, your throat feels scratchy, your nose is stopped up, your lungs want to—

A-A-A-CHOO!

All those symptoms add up to miserable. Oddly enough, those icky sensations are not actually caused by the *virus*. They are caused by *your own body*.

Remember how Netty Neutrophil flocked to the site of Stephanie Staph? Remember how antibodies swarmed in to snap on to Vera Virion? When a cold virus intrudes into your body, all those heroes are called in to hack, whack, and smack it.

The result is inflammation. Sure, that flood of defenders can fend off the virus, but there's a cost:

- with so many helpers, cells are crowded together = scratchy throat
- to get the helpers there, blood vessels expand = stuffy nose
- in all that pushing and shoving, nerve cells get triggered = *ACHOO!*

Thanks. No thanks.

In Bailey Bat, though, things can be different. Often, when Bailey gets infected with viruses—even serious, scary ones—there's less inflammation. And that's extra odd because Bailey's innate immune reaction to a virus is super strong. And in most mammals, that initial immune response kicks off the inflammation game.

Aaron and the team wanted to know why. They wanted to know how. They wanted to know what that difference might mean. So, they took a closer look at the Australian black flying fox, a bat as black as night with wings wider than a meter.

A CHILL PILL

The team zeroed in on NLRP3, a protein that plays a role in the immune reactions of mammals. They decided to compare the NLRP3 in bat cells with those in mouse cells and those in human cells.

STEP 1: Enlist the help of a few more friends: rabbits, goats, donkeys, and even horseradish. (Hey, you've got to get your lab material from somewhere.)

STEP 2: Grab a few gushie goodies from organs: brains, spleens, bone marrow, livers, kidneys, and intestines!

STEP 3-999: Perform the experiments: burst cells open, sling them in circles, and coax them to spew their cytoplasm.

After all that, Aaron and his associates crunched through the numbers on a computer and crafted some cool charts.

NLRP3 in Mouse Cells: NLRP3 in Bat Cells:

NO. NO. NO. The charts the team made weren't *quite* as cool as that, but they did help the team see that flying foxes make less NLRP3. Not only was there less of the protein, but the DNA had mutated.

And mutation offers *opportunities for change*. And change in an immune system offers *opportunities to survive* when everyone else withers.

In most mammals, NLRP3 plays an important role in instigating inflammation. Think of a mountaintop rock. If it gets kicked, it crashes down.

BOP.

　　BOP. BOP.

　　　BOP-BOP-BOP.

　　　　BOP-BOP-BOP-BOP-BOP-BOP-BOP!!!

Like that rock, NLRP3 usually starts an inflammation avalanche. In bats, because there's less NLRP3, there's less inflammation.

Less inflammation = fewer sick symptoms.

If Bailey Bat is infected by Vinny Virus, but that infection isn't causing much inflammation, then it probably isn't causing any symptoms . . . maybe Bailey doesn't feel sick at all. Lucky mini mammals!

Aaron and his bat buddies weren't satisfied with finding this in one bat species. They aren't the kind of players who score a goal, then gloat in the glory. No, they tracked down, tested, and found this was true for tiny vesper bats, too. On top of that, in 10 different bat species, a whole family of genes had vanished!

POOF!

And what do those missing genes normally do? In mice and marsupials and humans, they code for other sensors that can also kick off inflammation.

All these results added up to one conclusion: in bat bodies, inflammation takes a chill pill. And that seems pretty important for a bat who gets plenty of virus exposure. A roost is a good place for germs to get around. Flying foxes aren't exactly skilled at social distancing.

Roost = 1,000 foxy friends

Plus, flying foxes don't stick to their own bubble. In one year, a single bat flitted 1,000 miles and hung out in 38 different roosts. An awesome opportunity for viruses to hitch a ride and spread the love!

The team's experiments have helped us understand how bats' superchill system helps them survive.

So, if I don't fan the flame of inflammation, you will chill out?

So, if I don't mess with your organs, you will chill out?

It's almost as if Bailey and Vinny have come to a truce. Kind of like with Victor Vulture, but in his story, we've only just found out that vultures live (peacefully?) with pathogens. With bats, we now know *how* they live peacefully with pathogens.

This mindboggling story rips the lid off the can of questions:

? How did this odd immune system evolve?

? Is this why bats can live so long?

? Does this have anything to do with why bats hardly ever get cancer?

? Do other animals have germs living peacefully inside them? Do people?

All this brings up a really big question: if a virus doesn't cause problems when it lives inside an animal, is it really a "pathogen"?

FORTUNATE FACT

Borrowing batty tricks, scientists are using our new knowledge about bat genes and proteins to help people with autoimmune and age-related diseases such as arthritis, Alzheimer's, and Parkinson's.

Annie Aphid sits, happily sucking sap from a pea plant. Little does Annie know that an infection is about to begin.

Wings whir. A black blur. The enemy lands a few steps away.

WASP!

Scientist sits, happily watching the battle begin. Little does Scientist know that an infection is about to save Annie Aphid's life.

This is a story of not one scientist, not two scientists, but many different scientists, in different labs, on different teams. This is a story of teamwork.

Let's start with Heather Henter. Heather studied wasps, specifically wasps that

**STAB—
JAB—
STING** an aphid.

Within a fraction of a second, the wasp is done. Then she's

gone, but she's left behind more than an ouchie. She's left behind an eggie. That's right, she lays her egg inside the abdomen of Annie Aphid. Annie's body becomes a living nursery.

ABDOMEN = the third body segment of an insect.

Mother Wasp's venom goes right to work. It dismantles Annie's nonessential organs and shuttles those nutrients off toward the egg. Once the egg hatches, the wasp larva starts sucking nutrients and oxygen directly out of Annie's tissues. Larry Larva releases ball-like teratocytes, large cells that roam the aphid's body, latch on to tissues, and start scarfing.

TERATOCYTES (tehr AAT oh siyts) = Latin for "monster cells."

Larry (and his terrorist teratocytes) don't attack the stomach or heart or brains—at least not yet. No, this toddler intends to keep Annie alive while dining on her insides.

Poor aphid. What did she do to deserve this? If her body can't fight back, soon her nonessential tissues will be devoured. Then the teratocytes will consume the very organs upon which Annie Aphid depends. Soon, Larry Larva will slurp and suck every last organ up. Annie will become nothing but an empty shell. An aphid . . .

MUMMY!

This wasp is a parasitoid, an insect that infects and then kills its host. As Heather watched those wasps, she noticed that not every aphid succumbed. Some aphids survived that egregious egg. What was their secret? Heather didn't find that answer, but she *did* find that if a mommy aphid could resist being infected by a wasp, her daughters could too. The trait could be passed from mother to daughter.

FUN FACT

Parasitic flies lay their eggs inside woolly bear caterpillars. What's a woolly bear to do? Munch a popcorn flower, which is packed with a poison that pummels the parasites.

SCIENTIST #2 (3, 4, AND MORE) ✺

Nancy Moran ran a team that studied symbiosis. Symbiosis is when two species live together in a very close relationship. Each organism is called a symbiont. A symbiotic relationship can be:

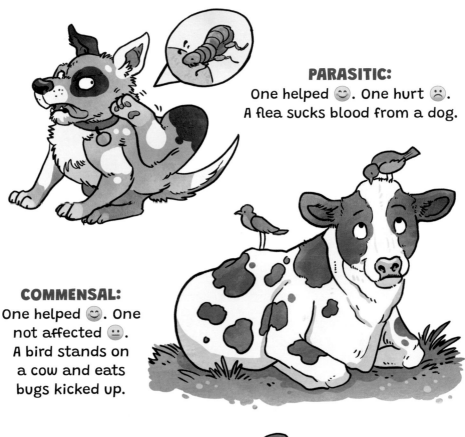

PARASITIC:
One helped 😊. One hurt ☹.
A flea sucks blood from a dog.

COMMENSAL:
One helped 😊. One not affected 😐.
A bird stands on a cow and eats bugs kicked up.

MUTUALIST:
Both helped 😊😊.
A bird cleans food from a crocodile's teeth.

Aphids, it turns out, are teeming with microscopic symbi-onts. We're not talking about a guest who happened to land in a mouth, got gulped into a gut, or washed into a wound. Scientific teams were finding symbionts thriving deep inside the tissues of aphids. Some sloshed in the blood-filled body cavity; some sat in specialized cells in the lining of the gut—they turned up in all kinds of odd places.

Scientists got extra curious about some rod-shaped bacteria that showed up in some, but not all, aphids. What were they? How did they get there? Why didn't the aphid's immune system kick them out? New tools let scientists spot three different types of these peg-like passengers, but they were so new to science that they didn't even have names. People simply called them U-, T-, or R-type bacteria.

Nancy, however, figured **SOMETHING** out.

She discovered that those symbionts were transferred from mother to daughter. We usually think of bacteria spreading from one living animal to another through a sneeze or a nuzzle or a guzzle of food. But unborn aphid eggs were already infected. Yikes! Mothers were infecting their babies! Looking even more closely, scientists realized that some bacteria can be transferred *only* from mother to child.

Working on two separate teams, in two separate labs, Nancy and Heather had discovered two odd aphid phenomena:

1. Some aphids inherit mysterious symbionts from their mamas.
2. Some aphids, once infected by a wasp, can miraculously shake off the infection.

Remember, this is a story about teamwork. Well, it goes beyond those two teams. Molly Hunter ran a lab studying those wasps. Molly and Nancy put their heads together and came up with an idea: what if those two phenomena were connected? What if the ability to resist infection is not an aphid thing, but a *symbiont* thing? What if, somehow, those symbionts were protecting the aphid from the wasp?

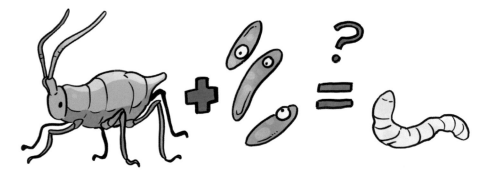

That idea seemed pretty radical. When Molly asked another insect scientist, he said there wasn't even a possibility symbionts could do that.

But . . .

. . . what if they could?

With no brain, a bacterium can't be smart enough to plan a way to protect its own home, but if a bacterium is dumb enough to kill off its host, then natural selection will likely nix its genes right out of existence.

The idea intrigued Molly. She shared it with a smart student who worked in her lab, Kerry Oliver.

Kerry never meant to spend his time with tweezers and little critters like insects and bacteria. No, Kerry was the kind of guy who liked thinking. Kerry liked big ideas. He was fascinated by natural selection. The simplicity and beauty of it mesmerized him. How had all the diversity of Kingdom Animalia come about from such simplicity?

Just take parasitoid wasps, for example. How had that complex life story come about? That puzzle had drawn Kerry to Molly's lab. Then she handed him this bewildering idea about bacteria. Could that be a piece of the puzzle? Suddenly, Kerry's mind was thinking of testing big ideas by playing with little critters.

LITTLE CRITTERS, BIG IDEAS

KERRY'S PLAN:

1. Find aphids infected and aphids uninfected with the bacteria.

2. Infect the uninfected with either U–, T–, or R-type bacteria.

3. Make sure each colony of newly infected aphids is pure.

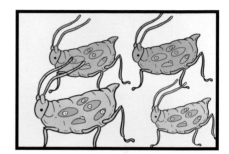

4. Let a wasp infect each aphid with an egg.

5. See who survives. See who becomes mummified.

Just like every plan, nothing is as simple as it sounds. There were twists and turns, needles and pipettes, and complicated steps. For Kerry, it was even a bit trickier. Before working with Molly, he had never set foot in a lab. How was he supposed to do fancy-schmancy lab work with no experience?

Well, luckily, this is **SCIENCE**! And scientists rarely work alone.

STEP 1 Scientists in Wisconsin, Arizona, and New York collected infected and uninfected aphids. Getting a few aphids was one thing; keeping them healthy was another. Plop them on a plant and the little buggers suck all the sap, destroying their food source. No problem: with a careful eye and attention to every detail, lab worker Kim Hammond kept the plants alive so the aphids could thrive.

The aphids helped, too. Mother aphids can clone themselves! A single Annie Aphid can produce up to 150 daughters, and each is an exact genetic match (symbionts included). A colony of aphid copies was just what Kerry needed.

STEP 2 How was Kerry supposed to give an aphid—an insect smaller than a grape seed—a shot of symbionts? Once again, he had help. There was Jake Russell, a student over in Nancy's lab. That's right. That *other* lab. #TeamNancy could have viewed #TeamMolly as the competition. The labs could have kept secrets and raced to find the answers first. But why not work together? They were, after all, after the same thing.

So, Kerry and Jake tackled the challenge together. Two other scientists, De-Qiao Chen and Alexander Purcell, had developed a technique for infecting aphids. Kerry and Jake borrowed their steps. Under a microscope: Hold one infected aphid still by sucking it onto the tip of a pipette. Slide the thinnest of needles into its belly and slurp up a bit of blood and bacteria. Stab that "donation" into the belly of an uninfected aphid.

PIPETTE
(piy PEHT) = a more precise version of an eyedropper.

STEP 3 A few years earlier, *another* scientist, Kary Mullis, had invented a new technique that revolutionized life science. Thanks to that, Kerry and Jake could speed-read the DNA and make sure each colony of aphids carried only the R-, T-, or U-type bacteria. Successfully infecting the aphids took them A YEAR AND A HALF. But, hey, they were committed to finding aphid answers.

STEP 4 Getting the wasp to lay her egg was the easy part— easy, that is, after you figure out how to rear and keep parasitoid wasps fat and happy and healthy enough to lay eggs . . . After that, Kerry put each aphid (some with each type of bacteria and some with no bacteria) on a potted plant and used a clear Solo cup to seal it off from the world.

STEP 5 Finally, it was time to count the mummies!

No R–Type Bacteria:
8 Survivors.

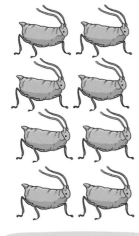

Infected by R–Type
Bacteria: 13 Survivors.

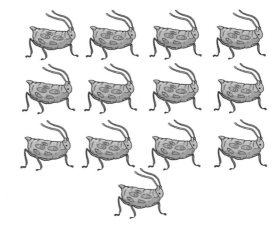

No T–Type Bacteria:
10 Survivors.

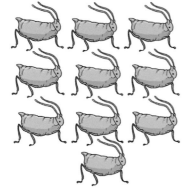

Infected by T–Type
Bacteria: 18 Survivors.

Symbionts as saviors! Although the test with the U-type bacteria didn't show any significant difference, aphids with R- or T-type bacteria had a much higher survival rate. Pea aphids, you had better lay out the welcome mat for bacteria.

Kerry (and every scientist who helped along the way) had made an astounding discovery. Bacterial infections can help aphids survive. If you were living inside an aphid, wouldn't you want the aphid to keep on living?

A discovery like that gets lots of attention. Soon, other scientists tested it out themselves. Yep, yep, yep. They found the same thing. They started asking more questions. And it began to dawn on Kerry and Nancy and Molly and many others that there was something more going on. Just like a set of nesting dolls, one discovery often sits inside another and another and another.

Meet *Hamiltonella defensa*, the name given to those T-types. Kerry kept following his questions about those little critters. In a second study, he saw that Hamilton could be a hero and protect 100 percent of the aphids. **WOW!**

Yet, it wasn't always so. Sometimes only 19 percent survived.

Hamilton, are you slacking on your defensive duties?

It took several more years and several more studies, but eventually Nancy and Molly and Kerry and all the others discovered the cause: yet another infection.

Meet Aphid Hero #2, who just so happens to be . . . a virus.

But this virus, called APSE, doesn't infect the aphid—well, not directly.

The virus infects the *bacteria*. Who knew that even bacteria can catch an infection?!

What Nancy's lab found was that if Annie Aphid is infected by Hamilton *and* if Hamilton is infected by APSE, Annie has a chance.

Without Hamilton, without APSE, bye-bye, Annie.

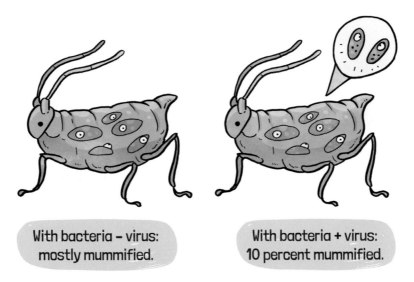

With bacteria – virus: mostly mummified.

With bacteria + virus: 10 percent mummified.

It turns out that APSE viruses code for toxins. Toxins that worm their way into wasp eggs. Toxins that make things not so nice for little wasp larvae. Sorry, Larry.

This story of teamwork—two germs (a virus and a bacterium) teaming up with an aphid—sounds too bizarre to be true. After all, a germ's got a job: Attack. Invade. Destroy. Right?

Maybe not.

Maybe a "germ" is no different from every other living organism. Maybe all a "germ" wants is a happy home, a way to survive, and the ability to pass its genes on to the next generation. Maybe teamwork makes that happen.

Pathogen or Pal?

IF germs are just trying to survive, if bacteria—even viruses—can help animals, why have humans been hacking and whacking and smacking them so much?

Ever since ancient days, people have feared the invisible. Before the invention of the microscope, people blamed diseases on bad air or seeds too small to see. Then in the 1600s, when Rome was struck with bubonic plague, a guy named Kircher slipped some blood under a scope, saw something squirmy, and proclaimed that microscopic critters caused the disease.

He wasn't wrong, but looking back on it today, we can guess that what he saw under his scope were probably blood cells. (Give him a break; this was way before you could Google an image.) Once scientists had scopes, others made similar discoveries. This idea became germ theory.

Once germ theory caught on, everyone started making assumptions. If it is itty-bitty, if it resembles an alien, if it looks sort of like something that hurt people in the past—

PLING!

Plop it in the mental bucket labeled "BAD!"

Slather up in antiseptic. Sanitize every surface. Pop a pill to kill, kill, kill! Those strategies saved lots of human lives. But they also sped up natural selection. Remember Stephanie Staph? Remember how some strains of staph became resistant to medicine? Our good intentions drove those microbes to change in a scary way.

But the microbes aren't the only things that have changed. *Our technology* has changed. New inventions let us look more closely at what's going on. *Our knowledge* has changed. Experiments have led us to new understandings. *Our perspectives* have changed. Now we realize things aren't always what they seem . . .

AN INVISIBILITY CLOAK

Take Stephanie Staph. Fifty years after *Staphylococcus aureus* was labeled a pathogen, someone realized it doesn't always cause symptoms. No lumps, bumps, or boils. No bulging blisters. No rotting flesh. This bacteria we thought was always a bully can actually live on us peacefully.

Name four of your friends. Staph likely lives in the nose or on the skin of one of them—and causes absolutely no harm!

When staph acts like a pathogen, most of its toxins come from genes that have jumped (like plasmids) into the bacteria.

Pathogenic staph, itself, is infected.

We now know that every bacterium is likely infected by at least one phage. A phage is a teeny-tiny virus. There are more phages than any other organism on Earth.

And in 2018, scientists found something even more astounding. When friendly staph lives on human skin, it fights off pathogenic staph! Are the bacteria trying to be good guests? Thinking of how to protect the host? Asking how they can help out? Of course not. No brain, no mouth, no matter—this microbe we thought was a pathogen can protect its host. Staph can be a mutualist.

"Playing nice" can be an effective way to survive and pass genes to the next generation. And that is, after all, all a microbe wants.

These days, everywhere we aim our scopes we are finding animals and bacteria making it work by working together . . .

To feast on favorite foods:

Eucalyptus leaves are toxic enough to kill most mammals.

Bacteria living in a koala's belly tame the toxins.

But a baby's gut is squeaky clean. No bacteria here!

Yum-yum from mum's bum-bum!

BACTERIAL BONANZA!

These leaves are all for us!

NOT-SO-FUN FACT

Eucalyptus oil is so toxic that if you swallowed a teaspoon of it, you might end up in a coma.

To fend off predators:

Snake sneaks.

Newt stands her ground.

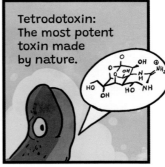

Tetrodotoxin: The most potent toxin made by nature.

Tetrodotoxin is made by four different bacteria on newt's skin.

Newt's not the only one who buddies up with bacteria for toxic benefits.

NOT-SO-FUN FACT

Tetrodotoxin is so strong that the dose from a single newt could kill 10–20 humans.

To fight off fungus:

Chytrid comes.

But little does chytrid know . . .

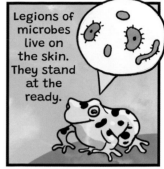

Legions of microbes live on the skin. They stand at the ready.

POP!

PUNCH!

PUNCH!

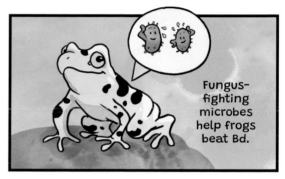

Fungus-fighting microbes help frogs beat Bd.

When it comes to beneficial bacteria infecting their bodies, animals have a thing or two to say about that:

"Come in!"

"Let me make you comfy!"

All across the animal kingdom, macro critters are inviting in micro critters. In the ocean, tiny hairs on a young bobtail squid wave in the water. They swish seawater, bringing in bacteria. *Won't you settle into this organ I've grown just for you?* Soon, 1,000,000 bacteria thrive inside. How do the bacteria pay Squid back for their comfy-cozy crib? They glow in the dark, giving him a special kind of camouflage.

No need to dive deep into the ocean to find such symbiosis. Simply take a peek in the toilet. Mixed in all your poo are the leftovers from the trillion or so bacteria who inhabit your own intestines.

Take a peek in your ear, eye, or belly button, where up to 100 trillion more bacteria thrive. And thank goodness they do. Without those bacterial buds, your body can't grow. It can't synthesize certain vitamins. It can't completely digest your dinner!

For example, sushi is yummy, but a human tummy can't turn seaweed into sugar. Normally, seaweed cruises right on through a gut and exits into the toilet. Many people in Japan, though, carry a bacterium with a unique bit of DNA. That DNA codes for a special enzyme to digest seaweed.

Symbiosis is simply astounding!

BEYOND TODAY'S BACTERIA

Now that our eyes have been opened by all this bacterial surprise, we've been willing to take a fresh look at other "germs." We now know viruses live peacefully in animal guts. Trees need fungi infecting their roots to absorb soil minerals. Even a wormy parasite can help its host. In the intestines of whitecheek sharks, a tapeworm slurps up food, but it also sucks in a whole bunch of heavy metals, taking in pollution that would have harmed its host.

Digging into the depths of DNA, scientists have been able to look back in time. They've spotted how ancient infections have done more than help an animal here and an animal there.

Germs have driven drastic changes within Kingdom Animalia.

Take aphids, for instance. Aphids are green. Well, most aphids are green. A few lucky aphids have DNA that makes them red. What color does a parasitic wasp spot best? Green. Guess who survives when Miss Wasp comes winging around?

And where did those aphids get that particular pigment? It didn't come from paint, powder, or colored pencils. It came from a fungus. Somewhere long, long ago, an aphid was infected by a fungus. Somehow a bit of fungal DNA got added into her genes and she passed it along to her kids.

And voilá, we have red aphids. Every time that rosy red makes an aphid invisible to a wasp, the aphid should shout:

Ancient infections for the win!

This stuff isn't limited to insects. Here's a startling story about microbes changing mammals. Technically, no mammal should be able to fly. Flight simply takes too much energy. It requires mitochondria to pump out tons of power. It generates too much heat. It creates too many free radicals.

Free radicals, floating freely in a body, can damage cells. Like the damage caused by a virus, that cellular damage generates inflammation. And you know *that* causes mammal immune systems to jump into action.

If any other mammal tried to fly, just putting out those flaming free radicals would exhaust the immune system. But a bat body? Thanks to viruses, bat genes know how to ignore inflammation. This led some scientists to a very intriguing idea: viruses drove bat bodies to ignore inflammation, and that allowed bats to develop flight!

Bizarre, right? Now, these scientists don't have proof—that

would take a time machine. What they are saying is: it's a possibility. And if we've learned one thing, it's that we should keep our minds open to possibilities.

Question: if microbes mattered so much in bat evolution, have they mattered so much in human evolution?

Yep. Approximately 240 million letters of our genetic code were gifts from ancient viruses. You read that right. Human DNA has viral DNA mixed into it. The DNA came from retroviruses, which are viruses that insert themselves into the genetic code of their hosts.

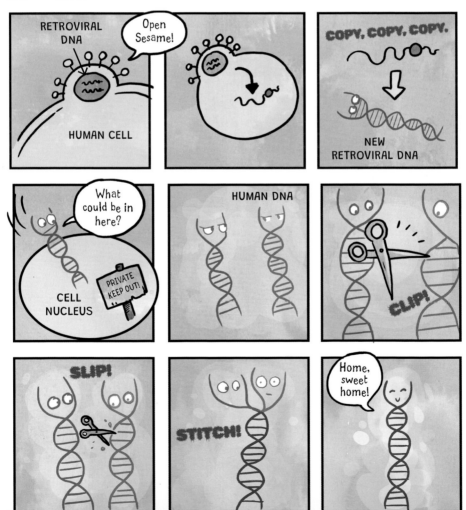

About 8 percent of the DNA in your cells came from ancient retroviral infections.

So then, why don't our cells look like viruses? Why don't they act like viruses? Like a list of spelling words that has been hand-copied a trillion times, most of that ancient viral code now contains so many errors it no longer spells anything useful.

ulcers erosion necrosis electrolytes
locusts ectotherm natural selection
pupa hydrophobic innate mutation

ulsers urosion nekrosis electrictes
loocusts ektothurm nateral section
poopa hydrofobic ennate muchation

uzlerz urosin nekros electrites
loocsts ektoturm naceral sectio
poopa hidrofobic ennace mucation

But some of it does.

Fifty million years ago, a retrovirus infected our ancestors. One stretch of code from that infection is used by our bodies to switch on innate immune reactions. When scientists removed that viral code from human cells, Mac the Macrophage became pretty useless. Ironically, DNA from an ancient virus is what our bodies depend on to fight modern viruses.

It's almost like ancient infections have driven evolution.

IRONIC = opposite from what is expected.

MIGHTY MITOCHONDRIA

Dial your time machine back even farther, way back to when Earth was still young. Before people, before dinosaurs, before Animalia even existed. Back 3 billion or so years ago, when microbes were the only form of life.

They were simple cells. No brains. No legs. Not even a nucleus. Nothing as complex as the simplest animal cell. Never mind the advanced systems needed for ants to make acid, gators to axe bacteria, camels to cancel a virus—how did that simple cell become an animal cell with organelles?

Two billion or so years ago,

- in an ancient barren sea,

a simple, single-celled someone drifted aimlessly.

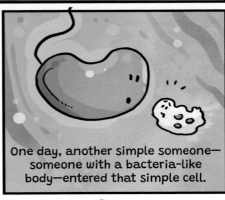

One day, another simple someone— someone with a bacteria-like body—entered that simple cell.

Why did it enter?

How did it enter? We will never know.

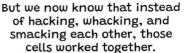

But we now know that instead of hacking, whacking, and smacking each other, those cells worked together.

That infection created something new:

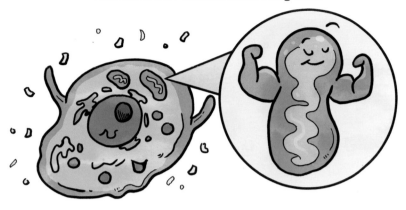

the mighty mitochondria. The powerhouse of animal cells.

We now understand that *every* cell inside *every* animal in *every* place on Earth—in a buzzard's beak, a chimp's cheek, a two-legged's tongue—exists thanks to an ancient microbe. An infection that changed life on Earth forever.

It's like this whole marvelous thing we call LIFE should thank the microbes.

Ever since the beginning of life—and in every eon along the way—"germs" have tackled a giant job. Infection after infection, germs nudged species toward better survival strategies. Germs coaxed the tree of life to branch into unknown lands. Germs empowered Kingdom Animalia to fill our planet with AWESOME!

More Super Symbionts

Other terrific examples of teamwork:

* The bacteria clostridia infect human bodies as soon as we are born. Some clostridia can cause harm, but many are our friends. One type that lives in our lungs gives the flu virus a one-two punch. One that lives in our liver improves our immune cells' ability to tackle a tumor.

* Ticks carry (and spread) bacteria, including the one that causes Lyme disease. Don't blame the tick; she never volunteered for that job. But if a western fence lizard is around, the tick may get lucky. If the tick gulps lizard blood into her gut, a pathogen-fighting protein from the blood will kill that bacteria and clear up her infection!

* A mother Mabuya skink doesn't lay eggs like every other kind of lizard. She holds her babies safe inside her body like a mammal. Why doesn't her immune system see those babies as foreigners and kick them out? Their cells have a protein that tricks Mom's cells into letting them in. Where did the code for that protein come from? An ancient retrovirus, of course.

✳ Want wings? Pea aphids normally don't have wings. When a pea plant gets crowded, it would be great for aphids to spread to a neighboring plant, but little legs can't carry them that far. Fortunately, genes from a plant virus give them the ability to turn on wing-making genes. Then, their kids can fly, helping both the aphids and the virus spread to new lands.

✳ Aphids can't seem to get enough of symbionts. Yet another bacterial BFF helps them make food. The sap aphids suck contains sugar but no protein. In any animal body, no protein = no growth. So, aphids grow special cells, think of them as comfy couches, where the bacterium *Buchnera* resides. *Buchnera* knits bits from the sap together to make the building blocks for protein. The aphid and bacteria are dependent on one another. Over the past 160 million years, they have evolved together.

These discoveries have opened our minds to even more options. What might we discover next? What might *you* discover next?

Acknowledgments

During the tragedies of the COVID-19 pandemic, I needed a way to understand things, so I turned to nature. Animals always help me make sense of my world. I thought I would just find a whole lot of fun—amazing adaptations, high-speed healing, icky but awesome immune responses . . . and I did, but I found much more. I kept bumping into stories of scientists changing the way we think about the world. I owe them my deepest gratitude for making this book—and this new understanding—possible.

Special thanks to these scientists: Mike Huffman, Cori Richards-Zawacki, Christopher Pull, Mark Merchant, Gary Graves, Serge Muyldermans, Aaron Irving, Molly Hunter, and Kerry Oliver. These writing friends: Jamie Dodson, Jared Austin, Jenna Grodzicki, Mary Kay Carson, Melissa Stewart, Nellie Maulsby, Rebecca Hirsch, and Tina Cho. Plus these book folks: awesome agents Rubin Pfeffer and Amy Thrall Flynn; enthusiastic editors Megan Abbate, Mary Kate Castellani, Diane Aronson, and Susan Dobinick; careful copy editor Sandra Smith; precise proofreader Lara Kennedy; detailed designers Kay Petronio and Yelena Safronova; collaborative creative director Donna Mark; magical marketers Beth Eller and Kathleen Morandini; and the rest of the terrific team at Bloomsbury Children's Books!

Selected Sources

Introduction

Hart, Benjamin L., and Lynette A. Hart. "How Mammals Stay Healthy in Nature: The Evolution of Behaviours to Avoid Parasites and Pathogens." *Philosophical Transactions of the Royal Society B: Biological Sciences* 373, no. 1751 (June 4, 2018): 205–214. doi:10.1098/rstb.2017.0205. NCBI.

Chapter 1: A Chimpanzee Pharmacy

Huffman, Michael A., and Heather Montgomery. "Chimp Self-Medication." Interview by author. June 8, 2020.

Huffman, M. A., and J. M. Caton. "Self-Induced Increase of Gut Motility and the Control of Parasitic Infections in Wild Chimpanzee." *International Journal of Primatology* 22, no. 3 (June 2001): 329–46. doi:10.1023/a:1010734310002.

Huffman, Michael A., and Mohamedi Seifu. "Observations on the Illness and Consumption of a Possibly Medicinal Plant Vernonia Amygdalina (Del.), by a Wild Chimpanzee in the Mahale Mountains National Park, Tanzania." *Primates* 30, no. 1 (1989): 51–63. doi:10.1007/bf02381210.

A Study of Primate Self-Medication: A Collection of Multidisciplinary Research Work by Members of the C. H. I. M. P. P. Group (the First 18 Years, 1987–2005). Edited by Michael

Huffman (2005). https://www.wrc.kyoto-u.ac.jp/en/members /huffman/CHIPP.html.

Velasquez-Manoff, Moises. "The Self-Medicating Animal," *New York Times*, May 18, 2017. www.nytimes.com/2017/05/18/magazine /the-self-medicating-animal.html.

Chapter 2: A Frog and a Fever

Richards-Zawacki, Corinne L. "Thermoregulatory Behaviour Affects Prevalence of Chytrid Fungal Infection in a Wild Population of Panamanian Golden Frogs." *Proceedings of the Royal Society B: Biological Sciences* 277, no. 1681 (2009): 519–28. doi:10.1098 /rspb.2009.1656.

Richards-Zawacki, Corinne L., and Heather Montgomery. "Behavioral Fever Information for a Children's Book." Interview by author. September 1, 2020.

Sauer, Erin L., et al. "Variation in Individual Temperature Preferences, Not Behavioural Fever, Affects Susceptibility to Chytridiomycosis in Amphibians." *Proceedings of the Royal Society B: Biological Sciences* 285, no. 1885 (2018): 1111–17. doi:10.1098/rspb.2018.1111.

Voyles, Jamie, et al. "Shifts in Disease Dynamics in a Tropical Amphibian Assemblage Are Not Due to Pathogen Attenuation." *Science* 359, no. 6383 (2018): 1517–19. doi:10.1126/science.aao4806.

Chapter 3: Awesome Ant Adaptations

Cremer, Sylvia, and Michael Sixt. "Analogies in the Evolution of Individual and Social Immunity." *Philosophical Transactions of the Royal Society B: Biological Sciences* 364, no. 1513 (2008): 129–42. doi:10.1098/rstb.2008.0166.

Pull, Christopher. "How Do Ants Stop Diseases Spreading?" *Science Features | Naked Scientists*. University of Cambridge. Mar 8, 2018. www.thenakedscientists.com/articles/science-features/how-do -ants-stop-diseases-spreading.

Pull, Christopher. "Evolution Montpellier 2018." programme .europa-organisation.com/slides/programme

_jointCongressEvolBiology-2018/webconf/350_19082018_1400
_berlioz_Christopher_Pull_47/index.html?fbclid=IwAR04
-5Qko0d_Ga_9fvfAYMHOcpHISHh5S_PVOfqc6LBUG4FE9
_k8SdE8DPc.

Pull, Christopher, et al. "Destructive Disinfection of Infected Brood
Prevents Systemic Disease Spread in Ant Colonies." eLife 7 (2018):
e32073. doi.org/10.7554/3Life.32073.

Chapter 4: Gator Aid

"11-14-Inside McNeese: Alligator Man: Mark Merchant."
Performance by Dee Myers and Mark Merchant. YouTube.
MnNeese State University. November 14, 2008. www.youtube
.com/watch?v=nZquXc0Hkjg.

Buchan, Kyle D., et al. "*Staphylococcus Aureus*: Setting Its Sights
on the Human Innate Immune System." *Microbiology* 165, no. 4
(2019): 367–85. doi:10.1099/mic.0.000759.

Schnoor, Michael, et al. "The Extravasation Cascade Revisited
from a Neutrophil Perspective." *Current Opinion in Physiology* 19
(January 2021): 119–28. doi:10.1016/j.cophys.2020.09.014.

Chapter 5: Buzzard Buddies?

Blumstein, Daniel T., et al. "A Systematic Review of Carrion Eaters'
Adaptations to Avoid Sickness." *Journal of Wildlife Diseases* 53,
no. 3 (July 1, 2017): 577. BioOne. doi:10.7589/2016-07-162.

"C. Perfringens." Centers for Disease Control and Prevention.
January 8, 2021. www.cdc
.gov/foodsafety/diseases/clostridium-perfringens
.html?CDC_AA_refVal=https%3A%2F%2Fwww.cdc
.gov%2Ffeatures%2Fclostridiumperfringens%2Findex.html.

Graves, Gary R. "Field Measurements of Gastrointestinal PH of New
World Vultures in Guyana." *Journal of Raptor Research* 51, no. 4
(December 1, 2017): 465–69. doi:10.3356/jrr-16-62.1.

Graves, Gary R., and Heather Montgomery. "Vulture Bacteria."
Interview by author. January 10, 2021.

Roggenbuck, Michael, et al. "The Microbiome of New World

Vultures." *Nature Communications* 5 (November 25, 2014). doi:https://doi.org/10.1038/ncomms6498.

Chapter 6: One Hump

Hamers-Casterman, C., et al. "Naturally Occurring Antibodies Devoid of Light Chains." *Nature* 363, no. 6428 (1993): 446–48. doi:10.1038/363446a0.

Moelling, Karin. "Viruses More Friends Than Foes." *Electroanalysis* 32, no. 4 (November 26, 2019): 669–73. doi:10.1002 /elan.201900604.

Montgomery, Heather, and Serge Muyldermans. "Camel Nanobodies." Interview by author. September 13, 2021.

Chapter 7: Bat Bodies

Ahn, Matae, et al. "Dampened NLRP3-Mediated Inflammation in Bats and Implications for a Special Viral Reservoir Host." *Nature Microbiology* 4, no. 5 (2019): 789–99. doi:10.1038/s41564-019-0371-3.

———. "Unique Loss of the PYHIN Gene Family in Bats Amongst Mammals: Implications for Inflammasome Sensing." *Scientific Reports* 6, no. 21722 (February 24, 2016). doi.org/10.1038/ srep21722.

Ehrenberg, Rachel. "The Bat-Virus Détente." *Knowable Magazine | Annual Reviews* (July 19, 2020). knowablemagazine.org/article /health-disease/2020/why-do-bats-have-so-many-viruses.

Irving, Aaron Trent, and HeatherMontgomery. "Bat Immune Systems." Interview by author. July 8, 2020.

Chapter 8: Aphid Magic

Gao, Fei, et al. "Cotesia Vestalis Teratocytes Express a Diversity of Genes and Exhibit Novel Immune Functions in Parasitism." *Scientific Reports* 6, no. 1 (2016). doi:10.1038/srep26967.

Oliver, K. M., et al. "Variation in Resistance to Parasitism in Aphids Is Due to Symbionts Not Host Genotype." *Proceedings of the National Academy of Sciences* 102, no. 36 (2005): 12795–12800. doi:10.1073/pnas.0506131102.

"A Toxin a Day Keeps the Maggots Away." *Science*, March 13, 2009. www.science.org/content/article/toxin-day-keeps-maggots-away.

Conclusion: Pathogen or Pal?

Malek, M., et al. "Parasites as Heavy Metal Bioindicators in the Shark Carcharhinus Dussumieri from the Persian Gulf." *Parasitology* 134, no. 7 (2007): 1053–56. doi:10.1017/s0031182007002508.

O'Shea, Thomas J., et al. "Bat Flight and Zoonotic Viruses." *Emerging Infectious Diseases* 20, no. 5 (May 2014): 741–45. doi:10.3201/eid2005.130539.

"Virus Genes Help Determine If Pea Aphids Get Their Wings." *ScienceDaily*, June 14, 2019. www.sciencedaily.com/releases/2019/06/190614111919.htm.

Vosseberg, Julian, et al. "Timing the Origin of Eukaryotic Cellular Complexity with Ancient Duplications." *Nature Ecology & Evolution* 5, no. 1 (2020): 92–100. PubMed. doi:10.1038/s41559-020-01320-z.

Index